COLORFULL

FOREWORD BY RICHARD DAVIS, CEO Make-A-Wish® America

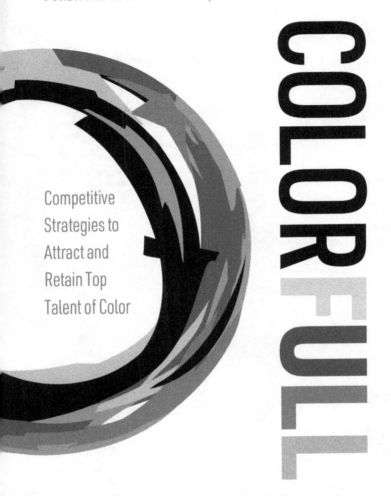

COLORFULL

Competitive
Strategies to
Attract and
Retain Top
Talent of Color

SHARON SMITH-AKINSANYA

NEW YORK

LONDON • NASHVILLE • MELBOURNE • VANCOUVER

COLORFULL

Competitive Strategies to Attract and Retain Top Talent of Color

© 2021 Sharon Smith-Akinsanya

Published in New York, New York, by Morgan James Publishing. Morgan James is a trademark of Morgan James, LLC. www.MorganJamesPublishing.com

ISBN 9781631951763 paperback
ISBN 9781631951770 eBook
ISBN 9781631951787 audio
Library of Congress Control Number: 2020937770

Cover and Interior Design by:
Chris Treccani
www.3dogcreative.net

Morgan James is a proud partner of Habitat for Humanity Peninsula and Greater Williamsburg. Partners in building since 2006.

Get involved today! Visit
MorganJamesPublishing.com/giving-back

DEDICATION

This book is dedicated to my mom Amanda, my dad Al, my brother Gary, my dear friend Oscar, and my daughter Rae.

Rae, I hope this book will help create a space that allows you to bring your full, authentic self to work and offers you a seat at the table.

TABLE OF CONTENTS

FOREWORD

Full disclosure: I'm an older White guy. And like many older White guys, I've built my career by leveraging my own experiences and expertise. I've stuck to what I know and understand, and that's worked for me.

I'm the current CEO of a major nonprofit and former CEO of the fifth largest bank in the nation, which means I've spent many years surrounded by people who look and operate just like me. However, I am also keenly aware that when we meet and work with people who look different from us, we tend to expect those differences to be surface level. We assume that we have more in common than differences. While our intentions are good, we might not value the diversity of thought and working styles that stem from different life experiences.

This needs to change. Especially since the vast majority of people working for a corporation don't look (or operate) like the C-suite executives running the show.

Of course, leaders and CEOs of all stripes already know that diverse employee pools innovate more and perform better than homogeneous ones. We all agree that a variety of worker experiences and perspectives creates a stronger, more innovative and prosperous company. Yet, many leaders still have a gap in understanding around the needs of our employees of color. We know that supporting and engaging them is vital; but since their experiences are so different from ours, we struggle to optimize these relationships.

We also find it challenging to develop corporate boards that are just as diverse as our workforces. But, when we can successfully achieve our goal of creating a board that is comprised of people of color, we also create a foundation for our management teams to see and understand the importance of installing diverse leaders throughout the ranks. Board diversity needs to be "job one" for equity-minded leaders.

The underlying challenge is that even though we know and want to resolve these roadblocks to creating a workforce that is enriched by its diversity, finding the solutions creates uncertainty. We find ourselves trying to navigate in uncharted waters yet navigating them is something we must learn to do. To do it well, however, requires guidance from experts on how best to lead in this changing world—and why it's a smart decision.

While we know experience is the best teacher, the reality is most C-suite executives do not have much experience working for (or alongside) professionals of color. Even fewer are people of color themselves. **This book is here to help! It is specifically intended to help business leaders, just like you and me, jump**

ahead in the experience curve by hearing from others who have already lived it. They've made mistakes and learned lessons that only experience can teach. But they've prevailed and can now build a bridge for other leaders to cross. This book is for corporate executives who want to take that journey. Maybe they've already started down the diversity, equity, and inclusion path, but they know they are still far from the path's end. It's also for those who know they are ready but don't want to make avoidable missteps along the way.

CEOs don't need a new starting point. We need a new place to go to—we need a new ending point.

Enter Sharon Smith-Akinsanya.

Sharon has spent decades of her life teaching corporations to build stronger and more authentic relationships with talent of color, training CEOs and CHROs to see the world with different eyes. She saw a gap in the working world and stepped in to fill it with her creativity, business acumen, and empathy. She's entered countless uncomfortable conversations about race and equity, and has left them having forged lifelong partnerships.

I, myself, had one of these uncomfortable conversations with Sharon. I recall sitting with her at the Minneapolis Club, having a conversation with such intensity that the wait staff chose not to refill our water glasses. We both brought our energy and emotions to the table and shared our opposing perspectives with a healthy dose of candor. It was a challenging discussion for us both, but we respected each other enough to show up and do the work together. And that's Sharon through and through: fearless, dedicated, and boundlessly passionate about making the world a more equitable place.

Sharon has since expressed to me that our friendship and candid discussions opened her eyes to the key issues top executives face and struggle to conquer. My friendship with her has reinforced the values of being open and honest, especially in debating difficult topics—even when it's uncomfortable to do so.

In the business world, we talk about "proof of concept" as an essential benchmark. Sharon is "proof of concept" embodied. If she says she can show you how to attract, recruit, and retain professionals of color, you can take her word for it. I did.

By working with Sharon and my CHRO, we were able to set strategies and goals for the organization that accelerated its transformation. I was already inclined to lean into the important work of building equitable organizations from the top down, and working with Sharon helped me achieve the next level of success sooner and more completely. With Sharon's help, it became clear that diversity was only the start; creating an environment of true inclusion, engagement, and a sense of belonging is the endgame.

Sharon's philosophy guides her teachings. She provides tools to avoid the emotional trap that comes with reacting defensively to opposing viewpoints. Instead, she knows that leaders always make more headway by saying, "I've never looked at it that way. Thank you for giving me a new lens." And, this philosophy was embedded in the work we did together at my firm.

Sharon has successfully captured her core lessons in this unique and engaging book. By reading these six short, entertaining chapters, you'll get a glimpse of what it's like to have her as a DEI mentor. (Work with her in person, and you'll get the unvarnished truth—and you may even make an awesome new friend.)

Those of us in charge of hiring and promoting are the gatekeepers, the ones who aren't opening the doors at the right time or to the right applicants. The good news is that we're also the ones who have the power to break through that block, to change the flow, to release the stranglehold.

Because we tend to expect the experiences of others to mirror ours, we simply don't "open the aperture" for all the opportunities that are available for people of color.

That can change. It can change with us. We can dive into uncomfortable conversations, become more vulnerable on topics for which we aren't the expert—and we can learn what will work for all our people, including our diverse and innovative people. We can stop the unintentional exclusion of the talented professionals who have the power to transform our organizations.

Let's commit to making real change in our companies. As leaders, we'd never intentionally block anyone or anything that would make us better and our organizations stronger.

Let's commit to building a more equitable future together.

—**Richard K. Davis**, CEO,
Make-A-Wish˚ America.

ACKNOWLEDGMENTS

When you're tackling sensitive subjects like race, inclusivity, and equity (in or out of the workplace), you need advocates. When you're trying to change the world, helping people see the importance of building an equitable nation, and advocating for workplaces that are more COLORFULL, you need leaders and courageous people to speak up, take action, and force change. Doing this work takes a village, and I'm lucky to have one populated by truly phenomenal allies.

So, let me start by expressing my deepest love, devotion, and gratitude to my daughter, Rae Akinsanya. She inspires me every day, and I admire her more than I can express in words. My company, Rae Mackenzie Group, was named for her. She was just one year old when I started it, and it was my hope that by the time she was ready to join the workforce, its work would be obsolete. I had hoped that by the time Rae was a young adult, we would no longer be grappling with issues of diversity, equity, and inclusion. But she's 24 now, and we're still fighting.

And to my wonderful father, who has since passed, and my amazing mother, who raised me with so much wisdom and continues to pass along amazing insights every day. She once said to me, "Sharon, everybody's got the same 24 hours in a day. What are you going to do with your 24?" She said, "You can walk around soaking up oxygen, or you can be a force for good and make change and use your gifts." She said, "It'd be a sin not to use your gifts to make a difference in people's lives and in your community." So, I want to thank you, Mom, for your love, your advice, your sacrifice, your understanding, your being there through thick and thin, and for always believing that we can do this thing no matter what happens.

Thank you to my dear friend Pat McAdaragh, CEO of Midco, who believed in me and my vision for more inclusive workplaces in the Minnesota Region, and who has been with me every step of the way. Every time I speak or write about Pat, an ugly cry just flows.

I am so grateful to Richard Davis, CEO of Make-A-Wish® America, who has been incredibly influential among CEOs and other leaders in the Midwest and across the nation. He's widely respected for good reason. I'm proud to call him my friend, and I want to thank him for helping me talk about the importance of this work. And for putting pen to paper to write the inspiring foreword to my book.

Thank you to my best friend, Jennie Carlson, retired Chief Human Resources Officer at U.S. Bank, who led from the beginning on creating more racially inclusive workplaces. She's constantly providing me with valuable insights and advice, and her support encourages me to continue doing this work.

My sincerest appreciation goes out to the amazing Jay Lund, Chairman and CEO of Andersen Corporation, for writing the afterword for my book and for putting his heart and soul into taking a stand, for leading out loud, and for being a strong partner and advocate of the diversity, equity, and inclusion work at Andersen and in our region.

I want to thank Bryan Stevenson, author of *Just Mercy*, whom I've met twice and heard speak several times, and who instilled in me the importance of proximity. He taught me that we need to get close, get out of our comfort zones, and get to know one another. His work drove home the idea that we must get to know people who don't look like us, who don't make as much money as we do, who go to different churches, and who live in different neighborhoods. We need to be intentional about making new friends so we can learn from one another and have even more empathy.

I'd like to thank Janet Switzer, *New York Times* bestselling co-author of *Success Principles*, and author of *Instant Income*, for guiding me through the publishing process and introducing me to my publisher, Morgan James Publishing. Janet, you are a pro. You are an expert and an inspiration. Thank you for your guidance.

To my awesome team at Rae Mackenzie Group, including Kimberly Steward, Sandy Zeiszler, Khia Jackson, Patrick Brunelle, Oscar Esquivel, Ellie Vilendrer, Sam Gullickson, and Nehemiah Harvey. Thanks to every one of them for their professionalism, their dedication, and their flawless execution of the work that we do for our clients and our community at the Rae Mackenzie Group. We definitely punch above our weight, but we understand that we are counted on and must deliver results and make an impact. Thank you so much for your excellence and support.

And then to Sally McGraw, my awesome collaborator, who was a genius at helping me pull my thoughts together to get this book across the finish line so that we could share it with all of you. To Andrea Lehner, my editor, who made sure my ideas shined through on every page.

To my friend Kim Price, who always inspires me, and who helped me with my thinking around this book. And to the legendary Dr. Josie Johnson who continues to show me that one person can absolutely change the world and reminds me that I should never give up fighting for what is right.

Special thanks to all of the phenomenal CEOs, executives, and corporate leaders who gave their time and wisdom in the interviews you'll read throughout this book: Hubert Joly, Senior Lecturer at Harvard Business School, Former Chairman and CEO of Best Buy; Karen Richard, Senior Vice President and Chief

Human Resources Officer of Andersen Corporation, who has the unending courage to Lead Out Loud every day; Greg Cunningham, Senior Executive Vice President and Chief Equity and Inclusion Officer at U.S. Bank, and Reba Dominski, Executive Vice President, Chief Social Responsibility Officer, and President, U.S. Bank Foundation; James Burroughs II, Chief Equity and Inclusion Officer at Children's Minnesota; and the legendary Dr. Reatha Clark King, former Vice President of General Mills Corporation and former President, Executive Director, and Chairman of the Board of Trustees of the General Mills Foundation.

INTRODUCTION

Before we begin, let me tell you what you won't find in this book. You won't find blame, assumptions, or guilt. I'm not here to admonish, point fingers, or cast aspersions. There's enough of that happening in the world around us already. This book is about finding solutions. It's about elevating ourselves above emotions and letting down our defenses enough to have open, honest communication in order to solve a bigger problem—without judgment.

I'm telling you this now—at the very beginning—because I've seen far too many leaders freeze up for fear of saying the wrong thing. In today's climate, many well-intentioned leaders are so worried about having their words misconstrued that it becomes easier—safer, even—to stay silent.

So, let's start by acknowledging that issues of race and equity aren't just important, they are *complex* and often difficult to speak openly about. These issues are nuanced and emotional and downright scary to many people. I've spent two decades as a marketer working in the diversity, equity, and inclusion (DEI) space, and I've seen dozens of gifted leaders shy away from difficult yet important discussions, avoiding game-changing moves simply because they involved issues of race. This must change.

We need to feel comfortable talking openly about race, racism, diversity, and privilege. We need to be willing to make mistakes, learn, and move on. We need to listen to each other, praise heartfelt efforts to improve, and be brave together. We need to Lead Out Loud. That means doing what's right for our businesses instead of what's easy.

One of my goals for this book is to make conversations about diversity, equity, and inclusion less frightening and more constructive. My message may be honest and direct, but it is also meant to be empowering and supportive. I want to provide you with actionable advice you can share with your colleagues, advice you can successfully implement within your organization. My objective is to help you demystify and simplify how you can become a magnet in the marketplace by positioning and presenting your company in ways that attract professionals of color. This will enable you to build a workplace that is COLORFULL, and to dominate your competition when it comes to recruiting top talent of color.

Why should you trust me?

I get it. I'm asking you to take a deep dive into what can seem like dangerous waters. Before we move on, you need to know that reading what I have to share here will be worth your time. Let me first take a moment to tell you a little about myself, my background, and what I bring to the table.

For starters, I've been at this a long time. In 1997, I launched the Rae Mackenzie Group (RMG), a diversity-focused marketing firm that helped corporations connect meaningfully with consumers of color, tapping into the billions in buying power they wielded. (The firm is named for my daughter, Rae, a constant source of inspiration for me.) We also created events and connectivity for professionals of color in the Minneapolis-St. Paul region. RMG helped corporations, government agencies, and private sector employers build stronger relationships with Minnesota's communities of color, and it was a phenomenal success . . . that is, until the recession of 2008 hit.

I went from working with Target, American Family Insurance, and Verizon Wireless to watching my company collapse. Diversity marketing wasn't a priority in a down economy. Eventually, I had to pull my daughter from private school, the bank foreclosed on my home, my car exploded, and my mom, my daughter, and I were left looking for a permanent place to live.

But my determination was never shaken. Holding tight to my dream of a more equitable corporate landscape and leveraging my solid-gold professional network, I landed a job as Area Development Director at United Negro College Fund, and was later promoted to Regional Development Director. There, I raised more than $10 million and forged some key relationships over the course of my tenure, but rebuilding RMG was always in the back of my mind.

So, in 2017, I reopened my firm, eager to refocus on helping the region's top employers with strategies that give them a competitive edge when it comes to attracting and retaining professionals of color. Since then, I've added the People Of Color Career Fair™, People Of Color Careers™, and People Of Color Biz List™ to my roster of services, creating a bigger, better, stronger version of the company I launched all those years ago.

What's different this time around? RMG no longer focuses solely on leveraging the buying power of consumers of color. Instead, we advise corporations on how to beat their competition when it comes to attracting, recruiting, promoting, and retaining professionals of color. We remind them that marketing to, recruiting, retaining, and building stronger relationships with employees of color will make or break them, and that RMG can show them how to do it all. **Although my firm focuses on employers with nationwide impact that are headquartered in Minnesota, I strongly believe that by solving problems in my own backyard, I can help my clients lead by example everywhere.** I want the companies I support to become the rock stars of the diversity, equity, and inclusion world, showing other top corporations how it's done.

Now, I want to take what I've taught corporations through my one-on-one advising services—along with the lessons I've learned after two decades of having the tough conversations—and offer these strategies to a broader audience. I've seen how transformative those tough, honest conversations can be, and I know the single most important ingredient is a willingness to be open to the conversation. So, if you're ready to commit to meaningful change, I'll show you how to move the needle and create a competitive advantage for your organization.

Because I value your time, I'm not going to sugarcoat things or tiptoe around the difficult parts. I'll be straight and honest with you, but I can't promise everything I say will be easy to hear—sometimes the things that can help us the most are the hardest to hear. In my experience, it's imperative to get to the heart of hard subjects through candid, open discussion that's conducted with respect and honesty, trusting we won't be judged or ostracized for our missteps. Missteps are part of the learning process (for you, me, all of us). No one should be punished for blurting out the wrong thing or making the wrong call, especially if they were trying their hardest to be conscientious and respectful. Yes, we are going to face up to some tough stuff, but we'll do it together. As allies. I promise.

I know that, like me, you believe diversity, equity, and inclusion are the future. They are not nebulous, politically correct concepts that deserve lip service and nothing more. They comprise a strategy that every forward-thinking company must adopt in order to survive. Yet, many organizations that appear committed to DEI say they cannot find enough talent of color, while others struggle to keep their diverse employees happily employed.

Let's cut to the chase: the real DEI obstacles

So, where's the kink in the pipeline? Why are global organizations with gobs of resources somehow "unable" to hire and keep professionals of color?

I have the answer, but it's a tough one to hear: apathy.

If your company claims to be committed to increasing racial inclusion in the workplace yet fails to actually hire more professionals of color, someone somewhere isn't trying hard enough. Many organizations get stuck in the aspirational phase of diversification, and then get mired in the weeds and never end up making a substantive difference. When asked, they have a laundry list of similar frustrations and excuses.

Maybe your company has been down this road already. Perhaps you will recognize some of the same obstacles. While it can be frustrating to those involved who genuinely want to see change, the good news is that because the list of obstacles is relatively short, we know that most companies are getting stuck in the same areas. And, in my mind, that's a much easier problem to solve.

So, let's start by taking a look at the most common reasons I've encountered when talking with recruiters, hiring managers, CEOs, and CHROs about why their employee pools remain predominantly homogeneous— and the reasons why they need to reframe those problems into solutions ASAP.

EXCUSE: I want my company to be a meritocracy.

RESPONSE: And it should be. But here's the thing: qualified candidates of color are absolutely everywhere, hungry to apply for openings alongside their White counterparts. If you're not attracting them, that's on you. (Tips and solutions will be shared in chapter 2.)

EXCUSE: But my industry just doesn't attract talent of color.

RESPONSE: Then make it more attractive to talent of color! Actively build a company culture that visibly supports and promotes diverse employees. Get leaders to network more broadly and connect with outstanding candidates of color. Set up booths at career fairs specific to diverse populations. Make sure every job listing and external-facing promotional push includes imagery and text that's inclusive, welcoming, and reflective of the employee groups you want to attract. Every industry can and should attract, hire, and promote talent of color.

EXCUSE: It's so much more expensive to recruit candidates of color.

RESPONSE: Reaching candidates of color is no more costly than reaching White candidates. You simply need to know where to look.

As I said earlier, this book isn't about placing blame. I'm addressing these concerns upfront so we can dispel these myths and move more productively through the rest of this book. I'm not going to do you a disservice by enabling you to fall back on these fallacies. You've turned to me for solutions, so it's my job to be brutally honest about the factors that keep us from committing fully to diverse workplaces. If you or anyone in your organization has used these rationalizations in the past, that's perfectly fine; you're in good company. But now that you've cracked open this book, it's time to abandon those excuses and get down to work.

Diversify and include, or fall behind and lose money

Getting down to work means fostering a corporate culture of inclusion from the top down and moving the needle forward for professionals of color. It means being brave enough to make the occasional mistake, knowing that our efforts will have a positive impact in the end. And here's why this work we are "getting down to" matters so much:

- By 2042, the United States will become a majority-minority nation, and studies have shown that diverse consumers are more likely to support companies that hire people of color.

- Currently, people of color in my home state of Minnesota face unemployment 2-4 times more often than their White counterparts, which means there's a HUGE pool of talented workers out there going untapped.
- *Dozens* of studies have shown that diverse companies perform better overall in terms of innovation, revenue generation, and more.
- According to research by Greater MSP, professionals of color are 77 percent more likely to leave the Minnesota region because of lack of culture connectivity.
- A workforce shortage is upon us. Companies that are unable to both attract and retain talent of color will struggle to remain competitive. And soon.

Sounds dire, right? Luckily, you're already ahead of the game. You're eager to learn how to transform your company for the better, and you're excited to embrace a future-focused workplace full of professionals of color. You're willing to make a few blunders if it means making your organization more equitable and welcoming. You're committed to doing what's right instead of what's easy.

And, I'm here with you. I'll guide you through tangible best practices and solid strategies that will help you cultivate an inclusive culture from recruitment through retention. In the chapters to come, I'll share my advice for shifting mindsets and adopting practices that make workplaces more equitable and welcoming. Some of this advice will be aimed squarely at you as an individual leader. For instance, I'll encourage you to forge personal relationships with people who are different from you and to mix up the people you include in your network. Some advice will be applicable to your company as a whole, including cultural shifts and recruitment practices. (One-size-fits-all advice never *really* fits anyone.) But I will show you the key changes you need to make to attract top talent of color.

You'll also find interviews with corporate leaders who have worked hard and learned tough lessons about the importance of doing diversity, recruiting, and inclusion right. Many of the changes I suggest in these pages may sound uncomfortable and challenging at first, but as you read through the interviews with your peers, you'll see how transformative those changes have been for them. My hope is that their examples will inspire you to follow their lead.

Ready to make attracting professionals of color an authentic core value in *your* company?

Just turn the page.

CHAPTER 1

A Homogenous Employee Base Will Kill Your Company Culture

I s diversity hiring all about optics? At this point, most corporate leaders know the answer to this question, but let's have a quick refresher.

The short answer is NO, it's not just optics. Diverse employee populations make companies stronger and more resilient.

A longer answer is that there's no doubt hiring talent of color and mindfully transforming your organization into a diverse workplace makes you look good. And, let's be honest; looking good is important! Public perception is part of brand equity, and making business choices that secure your reputation as a forward-thinking, modern company is just common sense.

However, optics are just one tiny, relatively insignificant piece of the diversity, equity, and inclusion puzzle.

A 2018 study by McKinsey & Company found that diverse companies are better able to hire top talent, improve customer opinions, and boost employee satisfaction, all of which create a cycle of increasing returns.[1] Survey researcher and polling expert Tom Webster of Edison Research adds that homogeneous companies may fail to recognize customer needs, saying, "If you're at a company, or you're running a company, and you literally don't know anybody that voted for Hillary or voted for Trump . . . I would submit that you have some issues with understanding customers."[2] A recent Boston Consulting Group study found that organizations with diverse management and leadership teams bring in 19 percent higher revenues than their

---

1   Hunt, Vivian. "Why Diversity Matters." McKinsey & Company. https://www.mckinsey.com/business-functions/ organization/our-insights/why-diversity-matters.

2   Altman, Ian. "5 Reasons Why Workplace Diversity Is Good For Business." Inc.com. Inc., March 15, 2017. https://www. inc.com/ian-altman/5-reasons-why-workplace-diversity-is- good-for-business.html.

less-diverse competitors.[3] Like I said: diverse teams lead to stronger, more resilient companies.

And, as former vice president of General Mills Corporation Dr. Reatha Clark King points out in chapter 5, a diverse employee pool also gives you access to *diversity of thought*. When you cultivate a workforce that comes from a variety of backgrounds, you bring a variety of experiences and perspectives to the table. Your company gets more ideas, more input, more suggestions. Diversity of thought is crucial to innovation.

Diverse companies are innovative

If you work in corporate America and have even a passing interest in DEI, you've likely heard about the diversity-innovation connection already. All the big research firms and many venerable universities have done studies linking diversity to innovation. As far back as 2013, *Harvard Business Review* published a study by the Center for Talent Innovation stating that diversity "unlocks innovation by creating an environment where 'outside the box' ideas are heard. When minorities form a critical mass and leaders value differences, all employees can find senior people to go to bat for compelling ideas

---

3   Rocío Lorenzo, Nicole Voigt, Miki Tsusaka, Matt Krentz, and Katie Abouzahr. "How Diverse Leadership Teams Boost Innovation." Boston Consulting Group, January 23, 2018. https://www.bcg.com/en-us/publications/2018/how-diverse-leadership-teams-boost-innovation.aspx.

and can persuade those in charge of budgets to deploy resources to develop those ideas."[4]

A more recent study, published in 2019 by Accenture, linked innovation to "a culture of equality," saying workplaces that help everyone advance to higher positions are more likely to spark innovation and growth.[5] And, there are many more studies spanning multiple decades, industries, and definitions of "diversity," that all draw the same conclusion: homogeneous workforces simply aren't as inventive and creative as diverse ones.

WHY SHOULD YOU CARE?

In today's global marketplace, a business that fails to innovate, stagnates and dies. The days of making tiny changes to the same old products and re-releasing them to eke out minor profits are OVER, my friends. We're living in the age of disruption, a time when the right rule-breaking innovation can create an entirely new market. (Think: Uber, Airbnb, Rent the Runway . . .) Today's innovation is big, bold, and risky. And, you need people with big, bold, risky mindsets to spark it inside your company.

---

4   Sylvia Ann Hewlett, Melinda Marshall, Laura Sherbin. "How Diversity Can Drive Innovation." Harvard Business Review, August 1, 2014. https://hbr.org/2013/12/how-diversity-can-drive-innovation.

5   Ellyn Shook, Julie Sweet. "Equality & Innovation in the Workplace." Accenture, March 8, 2019. https://www.accenture.com/us-en/about/inclusion-diversity/gender-equality-innovation-research.

Yes, it's true that diversity of thought can come from sources other than racial and ethnic diversity; people of different genders, ages, sexual orientations, political views, and religions also bring the gamut of viewpoints to your organization. But, bringing talent of color into the mix virtually guarantees egalitarian, equity-minded innovation: ideas that won't just expand your organization's offerings in exciting ways, but will also push those offerings to more people, different people, and populations you may never have thought to serve.

This is important because . . .

Diverse consumers support diverse companies

Nielsen has released a report titled, "Black Dollars Matter: The Sales Impact of Black Consumers." In it, they pointed out that consumers of color are loyal to companies willing to create products specifically for them, and that development efforts should be shifted accordingly.

"Black consumers are speaking directly to brands in unprecedented ways and achieving headline-making results. [In recent years,] popular brands witnessed the power of Black Twitter and the brand impact of socially conscious Black consumers. Through social media, Black consumers have brokered a seat at the table and are demanding that brands and

marketers speak to them in ways that resonate culturally and experientially—if these brands want their business."[6]

On top of that, Black consumer brand loyalty is linked to a company's perception as authentic, culturally relevant, and responsible. Plenty of modern consumers pledge to shop consciously, but consumers of color are up to 15 percent more likely to prioritize brand ideologies and principles than their total population counterparts.[7] They're also more likely to react vocally and publicly—leveraging social media to voice concerns—when a company makes a misguided or offensive choice.

Diverse consumers are values-based consumers, which means they're more likely to buy from organizations that employ diverse workforces. Need another reason to hire talent of color? Doing so will help you appeal to *customers* of color.

WHY SHOULD YOU CARE?

Because if you successfully court this large and growing group of consumers, it can send your profits through the roof.

---

6   "Black Impact: Consumer Categories Where African Americans Move Markets." Nielsen. https://www.nielsen. com/us/en/insights/article/2018/black-impact-consumer- categories-where-african-americans-move-markets/.

7   "Black Impact: Consumer Categories Where African Americans Move Markets." Nielsen. https://www.nielsen. com/us/en/insights/article/2018/black-impact-consumer- categories-where-african-americans-move-markets/.

Cheryl Grace, Senior Vice President of U.S. Strategic Community Alliances and Consumer Engagement at Nielsen, says, "Our research shows that Black consumer choices have a 'cool factor' that has created a halo effect, influencing not just consumers of color but the mainstream as well. These figures show that investment by multinational conglomerates in R&D to develop products and marketing that appeal to diverse consumers is, indeed, paying off handsomely."[8]

And what's one of the best ways to ideate, create, and market offerings that appeal to consumers of color? Hire talent of color. Brainstorm with and request candid input from your employees of color. Get as many creative, smart, insightful professionals of color into your workforce as possible so they can ensure you make the right choices in tailoring your products to them.

Non-White consumers are a growing population

Newsflash: The U.S. Census Bureau estimates the United States will be a multicultural majority nation by 2042. In just a few short years, African Americans, Asian Americans, and Hispanics together will comprise 50 percent or more of the total population.[9]

---

8   Ibid.
9   "The Database: Meeting Today's Multicultural Consumers." Nielsen, October 7, 2018. https://www.nielsen.com/us/en/insights/podcast/2018/the-database-meeting-todays-multicultural-consumers/.

Here's another statistic worth noting: consumers of color commanded $3.9 trillion in buying power as of 2019, and they will only gain more in the coming years.[10] Consumers of color are an influential, fast-growing, values-centric group that will shape the face of modern business. Period.

WHY SHOULD YOU CARE?

Ignoring a group with massive and ever-growing spending power is foolhardy. But, by embracing talent of color within your company, you will reach customers of color outside your company. More importantly, if you don't get on board, your competitors will . . . and you'll be dead in the water. (Tough love! It's the truth!)

The moral of this story is simple: organizations need to hire in ways that reflect the consumer populations they serve and what our world looks like. Corporations that value innovation, customer loyalty, and stronger ROIs must view DEI as a core value. Companies that want to succeed now and in the future will only do so by building diverse, multicultural workforces.

This isn't optics, people. This is survival.

---

10 "Minority Markets Have $3.9 Trillion Buying Power." Newswise, March 21, 2019. https://www.newswise.com/articles/minority-markets-have-3-9-trillion-buying-power.

Leading Out Loud Principle:

Embrace diversity at mission level

So, as a leader, how do you ensure that your company population is varied, heterogeneous, and diverse? How do you cultivate a diverse workforce that is smart, creative, and informed enough to reach an increasingly diverse consumer group?

Start at the top. Make sure every single leader understands the value and critical business importance of hiring, developing, and retaining talent of color.

A great way to ensure this value is truly embedded into your corporate DNA is to task the C-level with weaving diversity into the company vision (the world you want your company to create) and mission (what you do day-to-day to make that world possible). Vision and mission statements can be useless and meaningless phrases tacked to corporate corkboards and ignored; or, they can be living, breathing statements of values and goals. When crafted carefully, a resonant mission statement can be a reference point in every meeting and influencer in every decision. A quality vision will inspire employees and customers alike. And, if you weave in the vital importance of diversity, equity, and inclusion, these guiding principles will help keep everyone within your company aligned and united.

But don't stop there! Make sure the underlying benefits of a diverse company are discussed and reinforced. Leadership should be consistently reminded that diverse organizations are more profitable. All supervisors and executives should learn about the innovation-diversity link. Hiring and nurturing talent of color is, without a doubt, the right thing to do . . . but it's helpful to reinforce the moral imperative with a financial one. Diversity helps with optics and morale, but there are endless statistics proving that it also helps with fiscal success.

Finally, make sure that DEI is never treated as an afterthought. These topics are always germane, always morphing, and always deserving of reexamination. Cultivating talent of color cannot be a consideration only during hiring and annual reviews; it should be a year-round goal. Meeting the needs and valuing the input of employees of color shouldn't happen only when tensions rise; leadership should always have a finger on the pulse. Professionals of color become disenchanted with their employers when they feel tokenized, condescended to, or like they must make a huge stink in order to be heard. Embed the importance of diversity into your company's mission so your employees will see and feel how important it is, everywhere, every day.

Leading Out Loud Interview:
HUBERT JOLY, Senior Lecturer at Harvard Business School, Former Chairman and CEO of Best Buy

In any community, there are leaders who simply stand out. There are visionaries who become the go-to people, the influencers, the ones who lead other leaders. In the Twin Cities region, some of those leaders include

Richard Davis (whom you met in the foreword), Jay Lund (whom you'll meet in the afterword), and Hubert Joly (whom you're meeting right now!). Hubert is a total rock star, especially when it comes to matters of DEI.

Hubert is a dedicated advocate of "showing up." It's not unusual to see him out in the community, attending talks on criminal justice and vibrant multicultural events, often by himself. He's intellectually curious about what's going on around him, and he understands the importance of amplifying marginalized voices. I am consistently impressed by his ability to "walk the talk."

A few years back, Hubert and I had a frank and difficult conversation over a plate of macarons. (He is French, after all.) We were discussing whether or not Best Buy had the right people in the right positions, and he disagreed with my input. Vehemently. But he listened, and considered, and worked with me, and for that he has my eternal respect.

Hubert served as Best Buy's CEO for seven years; diversity was a top priority for him throughout his tenure. Every year he pushed himself as a leader to meet more and more ambitious goals, until about half of his direct reports and 40 percent of the company's board were women. (With the addition of Corie Barry, the company's new CEO and board member, women are now the board majority.) Hubert embraces a philosophy similar to that of Greg Cunningham (chapter 3); both leaders abide by the principle that true diversity and inclusion work means giving employees an environment where they can bring their whole selves to work. Due to this and other visionary work, Hubert was included on *CEOWORLD Magazine's* "Best CEOs In The World 2018."

When Hubert retired as CEO in June 2019, he advocated for Corie Barry to become his successor. I am so excited he made this choice, appointing the first female CEO of Best Buy. Hubert knew Corie would be a bold leader who would continue to champion DEI, and I am eager to see how she builds on his legacy. I'm honored to have had a chance to ask Hubert about the importance of diversity among employees and their shared vision for Best Buy's future.

Sharon: Hubert, why do you think so many companies struggle to get diversity, equity, and inclusion right? What's holding us back?

Hubert: First of all, I believe that in life, in general, and in business life, in particular, if you strive to recognize the challenge, you can finally start to address it. If you pretend there aren't any challenges, you'll never make progress. We have to recognize that this is hard stuff. This is deeply emotional work. There are decades, if not centuries, of cultural biases, particularly against people of color in this country—African Americans, specifically. Not long ago we had slavery. A few months ago, I was speaking to a young woman, and she told me her great-grandmother was a slave. Think about that timeline; slavery was not that long ago. The Civil Rights movement was not that long ago. These huge cultural forces are still at play, but so many people pretend that they're not. And that hurts our ability to move forward in unity. Whether we like it or not, this is within each of us. We can try to ignore it or assume it does not exist, but it does. And it has a lot of power because it is so deep.

Sharon: Absolutely.

Hubert: We have to recognize these are hard ideas and recognize that we're going to fumble. We're going to make mistakes, but we have to stick with it. It's like in any relationship. When you fumble, when it's difficult, you have to stick with it.

Sharon: I completely agree, and I am so glad that you're committed. I want to thank you so much for Leading Out Loud, because if we don't lead from the top, we do not move the needle forward at all on this issue. Can you say a bit more about why you decided to make diversity, equity, and inclusion integral to Best Buy's culture and hiring practices?

Hubert: Well, Sharon, it's very straightforward. We know from facts and observation and research that diverse teams are more effective. When you have diversity of talent, of backgrounds, and of experiences, you get a more effective outcome. Second, we have to match our customer base. The country is becoming very diverse, in particular from a color standpoint, but not just color. We just have to match the customer base.

Sharon: Absolutely.

Hubert: Third, from a talent acquisition standpoint, it would be crazy and counterproductive to limit ourselves to just one group or one type of individuals! Finally, from an inclusion standpoint, we want Best Buy to be a workplace and an environment where people feel included, feel that they can be the best version of themselves.

Sharon: As I work with some of America's top corporations, I know that it's critical for CEOs and C-suite executives to lead on this issue of diversity and inclusion. Why is it important to you to Lead Out Loud?

Hubert: There are two things I would highlight. One, if I want to make a difference, I need to make it a personal priority, and so that's what I did. The second reason is that when I think about my legacy, what I've left behind after leading Best Buy for seven years, I want it to include making a big difference from a diversity and inclusion standpoint. So, I'm all in. I'm committed.

Sharon: Many organizations get some resistance when leadership starts to roll out large-scale DEI initiatives. How did you work to get everybody on the same page, and make them see diversity, equity, and inclusion hiring as a business imperative?

Hubert: Well, it started with promotion choices. I believe that if you promote leaders who don't believe that having a diverse workforce is important, who don't believe that creating a sense of belonging is essential, then that's going to be a problem. I also created a four-pronged strategy that addressed diversity at the recruiting stage, asked employees to contribute to building an inclusive workplace, focused on diverse vendors, and committed to diversity-focused initiatives in our communities.

CHAPTER 2

"I Just Can't *Find* Any Qualified Professionals of Color"

et's talk about the pipeline.

Companies with homogeneous employee pools often say they *want* to hire more professionals of color, but darn it, they just can't seem to find any. These organizations claim they've searched for ages but come up empty-handed. They insist that the hiring pipeline for talent of color is bone-dry, and that their HR managers have no choice but to hire more White candidates.

This is despite ever-increasing numbers of professionals of color graduating with four-year degrees. Despite more and more people of color pursuing STEM and tech-centric careers. Despite a growing pool of educated, talented, eager diverse candidates . . . candidates that are somehow hidden in plain sight.

I'm poking fun here, but I do understand that this phenomenon is both real and frustrating. If you work for a company that's ready to commit to cultivating a more diverse workplace, but no one who applies to work there is a person of color, what do you do? If you need to fill a vacancy quickly, should the HR department hold up critical work to ensure you've screened enough candidates of color? If a hiring manager has looked everywhere she can think to look and has found the same, overwhelmingly White group of applicants, how should she move forward?

The answer might surprise you.

Safety in sameness

Spoiler alert: The answer is simple. Be intentional about making new friends that don't look like you." Let me explain.

I believe that we must expand our personal and professional networks. Experts say that more than 80 percent of our job openings are filled by networking and referrals. And, if you are a hiring manager or recruiter with a mostly White network, your workplace will continue to be staffed by people who look like you. I contend that in order to change our workplaces, we should work on being really intentional about making new friends with awesome people who don't look like us. Trust me when I tell you it will be a gamechanger for you, professionally and personally.

It's a decidedly human instinct to stick with what we know. We order the same sandwich at our favorite restaurant, go to the same church each week, and read every book our favorite author has written. We also gravitate toward *people* who share our interests and values: folks who have the same hobbies, live in our neighborhoods, share our political views. And, this need for familiarity leaks into our working lives, too. Which means **we build our professional networks from *people who look and act just like we do.***

In other words, our colleagues and LinkedIn connections are going to be very similar to ourselves. Women network with women, and men with men. Teachers network with other teachers, and CEOs with other CEOs. Knitters, musicians, martial artists, and gardeners seek out others who share those hobbies, unintentionally stacking their networks with those people. And yes, African Americans network among themselves, as do Latinx people, White people, and people of Asian descent. Instinctively, we want to surround ourselves with folks who understand us, individuals who can sympathize and relate to our professional and life experiences.

Although this may be natural and normal, it's a tendency that creates networks packed with similar-looking people. Organizational behavior expert Herminia Ibarra has said, "Left to our own devices . . . we produce networks that are 'just like me,' convenience networks."[11] And, she's right. Homogeneous networks may be natural and normal, but they're also the tiniest bit lazy. It's easier and more comfortable to build networks that make us feel accepted, understood, and like we belong. So, that's what we all do, even though it doesn't help us.

Because of this tendency toward narrow networking, White corporate leaders don't know how or where to find talent of color because they're looking within their own networks, which are brimming with other White people. In 2018, the Kapor Center for Social Impact released a study stating that if you're White, there's a 75 percent chance you don't have any people of color in your network.[12] So unless you're a Black C-level

11   Magliozzi, Devon. "Building Effective Networks: Nurturing Strategic Relationships, Especially for Women," The Clayman Institute for Gender Research, April 26, 2016, https://gender. stanford.edu/news-publications/gender-news/building-effective-networks-nurturing-strategic-relationships.

12   Allison Scott, Ph.D. et al. "The Leaky Tech Pipeline: A Comprehensive Framework for Understanding and Addressing the Lack of Diversity across the Tech Ecosystem," February 28, 2018, The Kapor Center for Social Impact, http://www.leakytechpipeline.com/wp-content/themes/kapor/pdf/KC18001_report_v6.pdf

executive, you will naturally struggle to find the diverse slate of candidates your company craves.

What if candidate search and selection is entrusted to HR? Same thing. Unless your HR department is brimming with talent of color, your reps will post open positions to websites they've used themselves, tap colleagues in their own networks, and thereby keep everything (unintentionally) homogeneous. Unless both HR and hiring managers are trained in DEI principles, they may make snap judgments based on candidate appearance, especially if candidates look markedly different from themselves.

So, if finding qualified professionals of color feels like looking for a needle in a haystack, you're probably looking in the wrong haystack! Stop looking for roses in a field planted with sunflowers. Stop assuming all people follow the same patterns and want the same things. Stop believing that diverse candidates will flock to your company if you aren't willing to step outside of your comfort zone.

Ever heard the saying, "If you want something you've never had, you have to do something you've never done."? We're entering that territory here. We've got to "get uncomfortable" if we truly want to make our organizations into diverse, inclusive, welcoming places.

5 ways to find stellar candidates of color

If the places you're looking aren't working, you must redirect your search altogether. This doesn't necessarily mean *more* work; it means different work. It's time to stop slinging spaghetti at the wall and home in on specific opportunities. Work smarter, not harder.

- **Attend events designed for professionals of color:** Take business cards and go to mixers, networking brunches, alumni events, and professional organizations that cater to talent of color. (These can be found on Facebook, LinkedIn, and through your employee resource groups, who should be connected to external professional organizations.) Actively search for the candidates you're seeking and share your mission. You'll be overwhelmed by the support you find by just getting out there. Even if you don't meet the exact person you're searching for at an event, chances are you'll still walk away with some solid leads.

- **Ask for help from current employees:** Leverage your company's own network. Ask everyone, including professionals of color already on the payroll, to explore any connections to individuals, organizations, or networks— personal or professional—that could help you find these candidates. This will not only create introductions, it will also raise the antennas of everyone in your workplace. You never know when an opportunity will arise for your team, so communicate what you're looking for and where you are in the process. Wear it like a badge in every setting that you're looking to attract more professionals of color.

- **Reach out to experts:** Connect with organizations of color and chief diversity officers at other companies or local colleges. Get them on the phone. Go to coffee. In addition to asking for recommendations today, create an open door to receive future referrals. Let them know what steps you're taking to nurture professionals of color in your workplace, and ask for advice there, too. If possible, leave that meeting by asking for recommendations for another person to contact, and then continue the search. Once you dig deeper, you just might find yourself delightfully inundated with ideal job applicants.

- **Seek websites and job boards tailored and marketed to candidates of color:** Generic job sites and career fairs have their uses, but when you're struggling to find professionals of color, it's time for a change. Go straight to the source. Post to Indeed and Glassdoor, but also Jopwell and DiversityJobs.com. Sponsor booths at job fairs hosted by Historically Black Colleges and Universities (HBCUs). By doing this, you'll be able to redirect all that energy you're putting into *finding* qualified talent of color toward *selecting* from a wide range of applicants.

- **Showcase diverse individuals on your website, profile, and marketing materials:** Are you showing up in the right way? Is your company profile attracting your dream candidates? Do applicants of color understand that your workplace is truly inclusive? Look over your corporate profiles and job postings to make sure they're sending the right messages. Add imagery showing people of color; use language that feels welcoming; include statements about your commitment to diversity. Make sure your images and positioning are culturally relevant; you don't want to be tone deaf here. If you have any doubts or feel unsure, ask for expert input and advice.

Remember, searching for the right candidate is akin to looking for the perfect professional match. Think of your closest, most significant relationships: your spouse, best friend, mentor. Chances are that you didn't find all these jewels in one place. Along the same lines, if you want to fill your company with perfectly qualified, naturally diverse employees, you need to mix up your search efforts. Cast wider nets; look outside your own network; get uncomfortable.

Try adding just a couple of these five tactics to your recruitment efforts; you'll be shocked by the shift of resumes on your desk.

Leading Out Loud Principle:
It starts at the top

If you're a CEO or high-ranking executive, you might think you can just send those five tips along to your HR department.

And you'd be wrong. Dead wrong.

Absolutely *no one* in your organization will buy into the importance of diversity if you have not bought in first. You've got to walk the talk and show everyone that you're dedicated to hiring more professionals of color. Make it crystal clear that diversity is a priority. How?

Don't just send an HR manager to those events designed for professionals of color; go yourself. Be the one meeting candidates and collecting business cards and telling the company story. You'll leave an amazing impression on the attendees; seeing a C-level exec at a networking event is rare, so everyone you meet will recognize your commitment to diverse hiring practices.

Don't broadcast messages about the company's diversity goals using a generic platform; send a personalized email from your own account. Yes, you should utilize internal networks to communicate a widespread desire to hire and retain talent of color . . . but do so strategically. Make it clear those messages don't come from some internal corporate machinery, they come from YOU.

Don't ask your assistant to reach out to leaders at other companies for help with recruitment; contact them yourself. Find and query DEI experts and HR managers at companies who are doing diversity the right way. Take them to lunch, pick their brains, share your findings with your entire executive team. Prove that this is a priority for you, as a leader.

And finally, don't just care about professionals of color during recruitment pushes—care every day. Keep diversity top-of-mind at all times and be vocal about it. Talk about it in all-hands meetings. Write about it in company newsletters. Speak about it in promotional videos.

In fact, when you attend networking events and meet with DEI experts, be vocal about that, too! Do some horn-tooting about your efforts so the entire workforce sees evidence of your commitment. Tweet about your activities, post to the company intranet, and explain what you've been up to and how it will lead to a more inclusive organization. Lead Out Loud in highly visible, public ways. Show everyone you mean what you say, and they'll follow suit.

Leading Out Loud Interview:

KAREN RICHARD, Senior Vice President and Chief Human Resources Officer, Andersen Corporation

When I first met Karen Richard, we were both exhausted. I'd been fighting hard to get a variety of corporate clients on board with making DEI a real priority, and she'd been working from within Andersen Corporation to make it a top priority. She wasn't sensing the level of passion for the work that she knew was critical to establish the buy in and investment necessary to make the required changes. We were both overwhelmed and frustrated when we sat down to lunch one day.

As we talked, she told me about her own experiences with prejudice, exclusion and being made to feel like an outsider when she was growing up. Karen's commitment to supporting people of color comes from a very personal, heartfelt place, as you'll learn in her interview below. Her challenging past has forged her into a smart, compassionate woman with a huge heart and a keen eye for injustice. And while she explained her situation, it became so clear that she'd already put a ton of hard work and passion into her efforts within the company! She was eager to learn and improve and do everything in her power to change attitudes about race and diversity. Recognizing her as a valuable ally in DEI work, I offered to step in to help her navigate the complexities of DEI in the workplace and drive meaningful change at Andersen.

We spoke with Andersen CEO Jay Lund and discussed the challenges Karen was facing in her work to create a more diverse and inclusive culture at Andersen. And as part of that discussion we made a very specific request: we asked him to step up and help drive change from his position as a leader and mentor. He immediately recognized the importance of his leadership in this journey, and we all agreed that the best next move for the company was to formalize Diversity, Equity and Inclusion as a strategic imperative under

Karen and appoint an inspiring leader to a highly visible DEI position. The company immediately promoted an internal candidate, and then later hired another DEI professional to round out the stellar diversity, equity, and inclusion leadership team.

Reinvigorated by the support she'd received from her CEO, Karen dove back into her work with a full heart. Today—due to Karen's tenacity and vision and Jay's support—Andersen is viewed as a trailblazer in diversity, equity, and inclusion.

Karen works hard to create a space for *every* professional to thrive, and she's effective at it because she understands that each individual is unique and recognizes their individual differences. She has told me that members of the leadership team are telling her they've never felt better working for Andersen than they do right now, and she's absolutely thrilled to hear it. She and her talented team focus on leaving their comfort zones and getting out into the community to make connections that close cultural gaps in the workplace. The work they're doing is as empathetic as it is effective.

To capture her insights for this book, I sat down with Karen to discuss how Andersen has worked to build a more diverse and inclusive workplace. We talked about equity and inclusion, the challenges and triumphs, how far Andersen has come, and how far they have left to go.

Sharon: Karen, my goodness, you have been busy putting pieces in place for a more transparent, open, inclusive, and diverse workplace. Why have you put this at the top of your to-do list? Why is this so important to you personally, and to the future of Andersen's workforce?

Karen: Yes, Sharon, we've been making great strides! But so many other companies are further along on this journey than Andersen, and we have a lot of work to do to catch up. We want to be sure we're not missing out on the amazing, diverse talent pool that we need to remain competitive and innovative. So, we interact with all interested candidates at the career fair and try to find matches to interview for all of our open professional jobs, with the goal of hiring at least five professionals of color from the biannual People Of Color Career Fair that your firm, Rae Mackenzie Group, produces.

Sharon: Can you tell me why creating more equitable and welcoming workplaces for all employees is so important to you on a personal level?

Karen: Well, I learned the importance of inclusion when I was just a kid. My family moved from the Twin Cities to the Iron Range in northern Minnesota, which turned out to be a very closed and unwelcoming place. Just about everyone in the Mesabi area was born and raised there, and they mistrusted outsiders, so I felt isolated and rejected. Just a few weeks after the move, I was at the playground hanging on the monkey bars and nearly got my hair pulled out by a local kid. Not exactly a warm welcome to the community!

This outsider treatment continued through high school, when I met and started dating the man who'd eventually become my husband, Bill Richard. He really helped me broaden my friend group. Most Iron Range residents are of European descent, but Bill's community college had a handful of students of color, and we all became close. We looked out for each other. I was so grateful to finally feel welcome and accepted, to feel like I could be myself and not worry about fitting in! Even today, I can remember how good that felt, after all those years.

Having moved to the region as a young White girl and having experienced outright hostility for being "different," I felt tremendous empathy for the students of color Bill and I befriended. Ever since then, I've known that absolutely no one should be made to feel shunned or excluded for any reason.

Sharon: When it comes to diversity and inclusion within Andersen Corporation, what inspired and motivated you to kick things into high gear?

Karen: From a personal perspective, it was just fundamentally the right thing to do! I'm fortunate to work in an organization that aligns with my values and has a longstanding commitment to creating a working environment that's welcoming to all people. Part of that commitment is cultivating an inclusive culture where everyone can bring 100 percent of themselves to work each day. We also work hard to make Andersen a place where employees feel comfortable having complex, sometimes difficult, conversations about diversity and inclusion, which is important because we live in a complex, divisive world right now.

Sharon: As we've often discussed, unless the CEO is fully on board and vocal and active on issues of diversity, it's incredibly difficult to get buy-in throughout the entire organization. Why do you think that is?

Karen: I believe that some employees are afraid of making mistakes, offending, or being judged if they're unsure of the overall corporate stance. And that stance comes from the top. Fortunately, at Andersen, our CEO, Jay Lund, speaks from his heart and believes in creating trusting environments where people can have tough conversations about diversity and inclusion. Jay led the Itasca CEO DEI Collaborative for a year, and I believe this helped create the space and the confidence he needed to really lead out loud on DEI. He's become a tremendous ally to everyone at the company who feels underrepresented or marginalized.

Sharon: So, what is Andersen doing to break down the barriers and get buy-in to get the work done? In other words, how do you attract, recruit, and retain? How do you ensure you can deliver a diverse slate of candidates to your business units?

Karen: Well, Sharon, as you know we've had a real challenge sourcing diverse slates of candidates in the past. We struggled for years to find the right source to help us identify a top pool of professionals of color. Then I attended my first People of Color Career Fair and POC Networking Breakfast last fall, and everything changed! Suddenly, all the candidates we had been tirelessly searching for were stopping by our booth and sharing their stories with us at our private networking breakfast. We subscribed to the POCCareers.com database following the event, and we use it for every professional job we source now. We are so grateful to have this resource, and our hiring managers are thrilled with our recruiters being able to deliver a diverse slate of candidates for their searches.

I know exactly how challenging it can feel to find and recruit talent of color when you work in HR at a large firm, but I also know that continuing to look is crucial. It's not enough to throw up your hands and say, "Oh well, I tried." You've got to connect with the right people and find the right resources, keep networking and digging until you find the places online and in your community where talent of color congregate. Then reach out, connect, build those relationships.

Sharon: When you think about the future of Andersen's workforce, can you picture an opportunity to hire more professionals of color who are also veterans, disabled, LGTBQ, Karen? Paint a picture of what your future workplace could look like.

Karen: We realize this is a journey and our work will never be done, which is why we we're building out our diversity, equity, and inclusion leadership team. This team is focused on engaging across Andersen, guiding our collective work to cultivate an environment that embraces diversity and promotes an open and welcoming community. My aspiration is that our work together will lead to a time when we have a workforce that resembles our customer base, a culture where everyone feels like they can bring 100 percent of themselves to work each day, and a greater Twin Cities' community where we no longer have an employment gap for people of color.

Sharon: Karen, you've been leading in this space, with a stellar reputation among your peers and leaders. In 2018 you hired Andersen's first Director of Diversity and Inclusion, and then more recently you added a Senior Director of Talent and Inclusion. Why was that so important to get done, and so quickly, too?

Karen: It's true! We promoted an internal professional of color to Director of Diversity and Inclusion in 2018, and then added an external hire, Tracey Gibson, who came on as our Senior Director of Talent and Inclusion to round out the team. Both were champions of diversity and inclusion initiatives in the community long before joining Andersen, so I knew they'd be instrumental in helping us fully realize our vision that everyone benefits from their association with Andersen. Tracey's leadership is particularly revolutionary since it combines talent acquisition and DEI to create greater synergy to accelerate our talent pipeline and DEI Strategy.

In terms of the speed, once we decided to create these positions, we knew we needed to get skilled leaders into place quickly. Now, Tracey leads the team responsible for partnering with leaders across the company to cultivate a work environment that embraces diversity and promotes an open and welcoming community.

Sharon: Why do you think we don't have more professionals of color in the C-suite and at the top levels of corporate America? Any plans for Andersen to address this?

Karen: This is a real issue, and one we are working to understand and improve. It has to start at the top to ensure that there is alignment, and also to drive the strategy. Phyllis Anderson, who is African American, is our first board member of color. She joined the Andersen Board of Directors just over a year ago and has been a tremendous asset. Her leadership has exemplified to the board that diversity in the boardroom drives richer conversations, more thought-provoking questions, and new ways of thinking about the business. We've also created high-level advocacy for diversity at all levels, which has already accelerated our progress of increasing the number of professionals of color we have in leadership.

Sharon: What advice would you give to other CHROs or executives hoping to cultivate more diverse workforces? What should they do, and what should they avoid doing, to find and attract talent of color?

Karen: It starts with culture first. If you don't have a culture of inclusion, then don't spend a lot of time and energy attracting and hiring diverse talent. At Andersen, our values are all about treating each other with dignity and respect. We live these values every day, and we model them from the top of the company to the front-line leaders with zero tolerance for misalignment.

Because we have a culture of inclusion and values that are reflective of treating all people with dignity and respect, we were ready to accelerate our diversity and inclusion journey in profound ways. Not only did our executives and leaders embrace this opportunity, but candidates who researched companies in advance sought Andersen Corporation out as an employer that embraces all people. In addition, we've quickly expanded our talent acquisition strategy to include the POCCareers.com and People of Color Career Fair databases, a variety of diverse career fairs, HBCUs, and we frequently tap into our diverse employee population for referrals. We have a long way to go, but we are making progress. And that is what this journey is all about!

CHAPTER 3

The Key to Attracting Qualified Professionals of Color

The crucial first step in hiring more professionals of color is to seek them out intentionally and actively. And, what's the best way to build on that momentum?

Make sure EVERY message you send tells them you *want* them, *welcome* them, and *value* them as unique individuals.

That means pushing beyond job description tweaks and recruitment material revisions, to overhauling company bios and profiles. It means ensuring any text or photo they might see conveys your commitment to equity and diversity. You want talent of color to receive a unified impression of your organization, and you want that impression to *prove* you're eager to hire and promote them.

You also want them to know that you value diversity beyond the surface level. No professional of color wants to be a token hire, forced to conform to a culture that punishes boat-rockers. So instead, **broadcast your desire to hire talented, innovative employees who bring their authentic selves to work**. Let applicants know that you value their perspectives, their individuality, and their creativity. Many companies overlook this key message when they reach out to talent of color, and that can be a deal-breaker. If your company declares loudly that it fosters an environment welcoming to a variety of backgrounds and perspectives, it will stand out in the best possible way.

Bottom line: If you're not showing up in the right way in public spaces, online, and in your marketing materials, no amount of targeted recruitment will help. You've got to send strategic, authentic messages about your company's priorities around diversity and inclusion.

Not sure where to start? Don't worry. I'll tell you exactly how to create company messaging that acts as a magnet for talent of color.

Welcome talent of color … just as they are

Later in this chapter you'll find a full-length interview with Greg Cunningham, U.S. Bank's Senior Executive Vice President and Chief Diversity Officer. Greg shares his early career experiences, telling us how his first few employers forced him to assimilate to rigid, unwelcoming company cultures. But here's a tidbit to get you started: it wasn't until he began to boldly express himself—sharing his experiences and perspectives as a man of color—that he realized exactly how suffocating those environments had been.

"One Monday morning I talked about seeing a movie with my family over the weekend and mentioned an idea from the movie that could relate to our business," Greg said. "It sparked conversation and ideas; it was then I learned that being myself and mustering the courage to bring my authentic self to work was essential."

Today, Greg is a vocal advocate for authenticity among talent of color and a champion of corporate cultures that encourage *all* employees to express themselves. Greg knows that when you create space for authenticity, productivity goes up, morale improves, teams become stronger, and employee loyalty skyrockets. Companies that hire professionals of color and then force them to assimilate in inauthentic, stifling ways quickly lose those professionals of color. Companies that truly value diverse thought and talent—and are vocal about it—attract and retain professionals of color.

So, your first order of business? Keep *acceptance* top-of-mind as you review and revise your messaging. When you speak to applicants of color, tell them in no uncertain terms that you expect them to bring their full, unique, authentic selves to work every single day. Do that, and you'll set yourself FAR apart from your competition.

Create a company profile with DEI at its heart

Next up? Align your profile with your values. Make it a beacon to professionals of color, encouraging them to bring their talents to your company, where they'll be respected, supported, and valued.

Of course, doing this is more challenging nowadays than it was just a decade or two ago.

In the past, your corporate profile was entirely under your control . . . but times have changed. Now you need to consider your website's "about" page, all your corporate social media bios, your company's LinkedIn page, personal LinkedIn pages, printed collateral that explains your organizational goals, and more. Yes, your company profile is an introduction to your business that lives on your own website, but its actual footprint is much larger. If you want to position your organization to attract professionals of color, you'll need to keep an eye on *every* aspect of your public presence.

The best way to ensure that every inch of your company profile is imbued with diversity-positive messaging is to **write a master profile that is dynamic,**

and let that master inform all other iterations. This master profile will likely live on your company site, where you'll have the space to include everything from details on your products and services, to organizational history, to leadership information, to noteworthy accomplishments. Create a rich, multifaceted narrative that showcases all aspects of your company's work and personality.

As you build it out, put your organization's inclusion policies front-and-center. Here are six aspects of your company's master profile that should reflect your dedication to building an inclusive and diverse organization:

SHARE YOUR DIVERSITY MISSION: Be sure to state you are an Equal Opportunity Employer, but don't stop there! **Talk about WHY your business is looking to attract more professionals of color**, and why you hope to promote them into leadership roles. Is it because your clients come from diverse backgrounds, and you want to reflect those customers' values? Do you have a specific department that would benefit from varied points of view? Do your people want to create a more dynamic culture within company walls? Simply saying that you're eager to hire talent of color is not enough. When jobseekers encounter your profile, they will want you to tell them why you need them, what you value about them, and how you plan to amplify their contributions and perspectives.

PROVE THAT YOU *ALREADY* VALUE TALENT OF COLOR:
Jobseekers of color seek out companies that actively support their current talent of color. **They want to know they'll be joining a firm that's already done some work to close the cultural gap**. So, tell them what you stand for, and how you're putting your values into action. Are you being inclusive at all levels, including leadership? How are employees of color being supported by your current systems and structures? Do you have employee network groups? Mentorships or sponsorships for talent of color? A current director of DEI? How is cultural connectivity *already* happening within your organization? Talk about this in your master profile.

DESCRIBE YOUR COMPANY CULTURE: Want more professionals of color to join your team? Share your story. Talk about your culture. Let applicants know what inspires your teams and how you're making a difference in your community. Explain how work gets done, but also describe how work-life balance is maintained. If you have innovative or unusual employee policies around working from home, or time off, or advancement opportunities, mention those. Again, merely stating that you hope to bring more talent of color into the fold won't trigger an avalanche of resumes. **You've got to show promising applicants why you're a top-notch employer, and why their perspectives and talents will be a perfect fit.** Let professionals of color who read your company profile feel excited about the possibilities, and help them imagine what their work life would be like if they choose to join you.

EMPHASIZE THAT YOU VALUE AUTHENTICITY: Some employers don't welcome professionals of color fully and wholly. After decades of half-hearted diversity hiring efforts based on stats, optics, and publicity needs, these jobseekers are wary. Many have taken jobs at firms that want them to adjust their appearance and dress, change their speech patterns, tone down their opinions, code-switch on command, and leave their true selves at home. **To attract the best and brightest talent of color, use your profile to explain how much you value honesty, expressiveness, varied opinions, and personal experiences.** Tell applicants that they are not just welcome but *encouraged* to bring their authentic selves to work every single day. Professionals of color know this kind of genuine acceptance is valuable and rare, so touting it is a fantastic way to pique their interest. (More on this from Greg toward the end of the chapter!)

USE IMAGES THAT REFLECT DIVERSITY: This may seem like a no-brainer, but many companies still miss the mark. If a young woman of color is curious about working at Company X, pulls up their "about us" page, and sees endless photos of middle-aged White men, she may feel unwelcome or excluded. If an older African American man is investigating Company Y, but every employee photo shows throngs of White twenty-somethings, he will look elsewhere. **Do the images you use in your company profile reflect the diversity you want to attract?** If you want professionals of color to feel welcome and accepted, pepper your profile with images showing your current employees of color. Choose warm, inviting photos that reflect your company's best self.

LEVERAGE TESTIMONIALS FROM CURRENT EMPLOYEES:
In many cases, user reviews and peer feedback are more meaningful to jobseekers than rubber-stamped company rhetoric. (Think about shopping online. We all read the customer reviews before clicking "buy," right? This is no different!) With that in mind, gather testimonials from current employees. Ask them to speak openly about what it's really like to work at your organization. And, **since you're eager to hire more professionals of color, interview professionals of color, and ask them to address the concerns of your ideal talent.** Aim for honesty, which may include a few opinions on weak spots and areas for improvement; this type of candor appeals to ALL applicants. Use pull-quotes, video footage, and blurbs from these testimonials wherever you can to give your profile a grounded, authentic feel.

Naturally, this master profile must be accurate and honest. If you *claim* to value diversity but fail to back up that claim with meaningful action, professionals of color will run for the hills. But if you make it clear that you are already supporting your talent of color, building in more opportunities of advancement, and valuing their input, you're on the right track.

Your leadership profile must ALSO reflect your values

The company's online footprint should be priority one: if it falls flat and disappoints applicants of color, you're sunk. However, **savvy jobseekers who are intrigued by your organization may dig deeper by reading individual leader profiles on LinkedIn or the corporate site.** When professionals of color are exploring their employment options, they want to know that company values run deep. If their research leads them to your online profiles and YOUR words don't support the company's values, that may raise a red flag.

As a leader, you undoubtedly have a packed schedule and little time to worry about tweaking your bio and online CV . . . but you need to *make* time. Your professional profile is a direct reflection of your career and accomplishments, so keep it up to date. Be genuine and honest about your leadership style, commitment to inclusion, and professional mission. Otherwise you risk letting talent of color walk away disappointed.

Need help making meaningful revisions? Here's your cheat sheet:

Step 1: Broadcast gravitas with a professional photo

A picture really is worth a thousand words, and you *don't* want any of those words to be "Yikes!" or "Ooh, bad hair day." If your headshot is messy or overly casual, it immediately gives the impression that you don't take your leadership profile seriously. You don't have to put on a suit and scowl into the camera, but you do have to hire a pro to make sure you look your absolute best. No arguments and no selfies. Just do it.

Step 2: Be sincere in your profile summary

A leader's summary shouldn't be a resume, or a blog post, or even a bio. This section of your profile is where you discuss your values, your formative experiences, and your interests as a leader. Readers will want to know how your leadership manifests within the organization, and how you use your influence. Applicants of color will want to see that inclusion and equity are so important to you that you mention them here! Talk about how you like your team to function, and what traits you seek in direct reports. Show them your true colors, and don't be boring!

Step 3: Surprise them in your experience descriptions

It's fine to list a few awards and accolades here, but to grab the attention of talent of color, dig deeper into the meaning of your work. If you describe projects or accomplishments, talk about why they were personally fulfilling. Explain why you admire certain diversity initiatives, and how you've changed your own priorities to focus on inclusion. This is where you can let people into your work and give them a glimpse behind the curtain. Don't be afraid to get a little vulnerable.

Next, **look beyond your profile pages, and consider how else your presence as a leader may show up online.** Make sure any search results related to your name and title are accurate and flattering. Remove any photos or videos that no longer align with the face you want to put forward, and upload refreshed content that shows the real you. It will take some time for the search engines to catch up, but controlling this information helps you control your online story.

Consider, too, drawing some hard lines between the media you use to communicate with friends and those you use in your professional life. It's perfectly fine to make your Facebook profile private so you can share family photos and circulate your favorite memes. You may want to reserve Twitter or Instagram for public viewing so jobseekers can learn more about your personality and views. If you do, limit your commentary and sharing to topics you'd discuss in the office or with your superiors. Never let your personal life seep into your professional social media presence.

Leading Out Loud Principle:
You must walk the talk

Building a company profile that emphasizes inclusion is vital. Using language and visuals that reflect a commitment to diversity will attract applicants of color who will make your company stronger. Your profile is a beacon, sending out signals that your organization is one of the good ones.

But a beacon is passive. To Lead Out Loud, you must be active.

As U.S. Bank's Greg Cunningham tells us later in this chapter, **you need to stand up and articulate WHY you**

believe inclusion is important at company meetings and keynotes. Keep an eye out for unnecessary policing of employees of color, and step in when you see that they're not being allowed to express themselves fully. When you give interviews about your organization, emphasize internal and external groups that support professionals of color, including employee resource groups, mentorships, and diversity councils. You need to ensure that your corporate board is brimming with professionals of color and members of underrepresented groups, so the people advising the top brass offer a truly wide variety of perspectives.

The profile is the beacon that attracts talent of color to your organization. But you, as a leader, are the advocate, the amplifier, the voice. DEI objectives should be aligned with organizational goals, and that alignment should be made clear internally and externally. Reinforcing that clarity falls squarely on your plate.

If you're serious about bringing professionals of color into your corporate family, you must walk the talk. You must be the one who brings to life the messages you craft for your company profile. You must enthusiastically and constantly prove that you'll back your diversity goals with resources, strategies, and meaningful actions.

Leading Out Loud Interview:
GREG CUNNINGHAM, Senior Executive Vice President and
Chief Diversity Officer, U.S. Bank
REBA DOMINSKI, Executive Vice President, Chief Social
Responsibility Officer, and President, U.S. Bank Foundation

Greg Cunningham leads all strategy, planning, and program activity for enterprise DEI at U.S. Bank, the fifth largest bank in the United States. He firmly believes that diversity and inclusion are defining characteristics of his company's culture—and it shows! Over the course of his tenure, he has implemented innovative initiatives and has made lasting change throughout the organization and the communities it serves. He's helped to create business resource groups, which connect employees who have similar backgrounds, experiences, or interests and their supporters. And, these groups have become a significant driver of engagement. He's made huge strides and has big plans for the years to come.

Greg's perspective on the importance of personal authenticity stems from his own experiences. He grew up in Pittsburgh during the racially charged 1970s, and he was one of the only African American kids at his private elementary school in the suburbs. **From the age of six, he felt like an outsider and constantly sought to mask his own identity to fit in**. As he grew up and entered the working world, this anxiety only grew. Writing about his experiences for the U.S. Bank website, he said, "I'd spend my Sunday nights thinking about how to best present a casual 30-second update during a weekly Monday morning staff meeting. I'd attempt to mirror everyone else's presentation style and content in hopes of fitting in and feeling as if I belonged. Ironically, all I felt was inadequate." The organizations that Greg worked for early in his career made it clear that this type of assimilation was expected, and that expressing himself as an individual was considered self-indulgent. He was told not to rock the boat.

Although Greg wasn't a rabble-rousing boat-rocker by nature, he felt stifled by these conformity-obsessed environments. So, over time, he sought work at companies that allowed him to stand tall in his identity, and that made all the difference. Now, as Chief Diversity Officer for the bank, he knows that mustering the courage to bring his authentic self to work is essential. As he speaks with leaders within the company and U.S. Bank employees across the nation, he encourages them to follow suit. He insists that organizations must value diversity of thought, experience, and perspective in addition to skin color. Greg knows that hiring professionals of color and asking them to dumb themselves down is worse than never hiring them in the first place.

Reba Dominski, Executive Vice President, Chief Social Responsibility Officer, and President of the U.S. Bank Foundation, helps lead the charge by working to close the gap between people and possibility. She does a stellar job of recognizing the importance of DEI work, while also acknowledging that we don't yet have all the answers. She helped create U.S. Bank's Community Advisory Committee, a 16-member nonprofit leadership group that ensures the bank's leaders are listening to community needs, today and for the future.

I had an engaging discussion with Greg and Reba about the importance of company culture and how creating a space where professionals of color can be their authentic selves will attract them to your company.

Sharon: Greg, you've gone above and beyond to transform U.S. Bank into a place where diverse employees can feel confident being themselves, expressing their views, and contributing fully to their teams. What does authenticity in the workplace mean to you?

Greg: I think of authenticity in terms of bravery, though it's never about an absence of fear or anxiety. It's more about **having a certain amount of courage that makes you unwilling to compromise who you are because of your environment.** It also helps you recognize that if you're forced to do that, you're in the wrong environment. One of the things I've learned over the years is the importance of audacity, and how much audacity it takes to bring your full self to the workplace. It's easier said than done, and it takes a long time. What has helped me reach that point myself is a willingness to fail. I've come to see that failure is rarely fatal, and that if I'm not failing, I'm not growing or pushing myself. When I'm shying away from failure, I'm not challenging myself to bring all my experiences, good and bad, into the workplace.

For years I was afraid to tell my story, to talk about growing up in a single-parent household with a mom who raised five kids in the inner city. I was always competing against people whom I perceived as having the right pedigree, as having gone to the right schools, and as having had the right upbringing. But eventually I realized that everything I'd been through—all my experiences, good and bad—created my true value. I had the perspective these corporations needed, and that was what separated me from everyone else. It wasn't until I had the audacity to be myself—to stop trying to talk like, dress like, walk like, perform like other people I thought were successful—that I could see it.

You can't resign yourself to living in a bubble where you're reluctant to tell your story or be vulnerable. If you don't tell your own story, other people will tell it for you. In the workplace, authenticity is what builds trust. If you are an authentic person, you invite people to break down barriers and see your perspective.

Sharon: Audacity is boldness, and I love that. But what exactly would you say to a professional of color who wants to be her authentic self, yet is afraid that her appearance or opinions or life experiences might hinder her ability to succeed within the company?

Greg: Your environment has to be a place that supports who you are. If that's not the case, you need to seek change. Some of the work we do in DEI at U.S. Bank is shifting the culture to one that embraces different perspectives and expressions of self as valuable and important. It starts with having a willingness to embrace that philosophy at the organizational level.

And for our part, employees of color need to get over the notion that the way we dress or wear our hair will make us unwelcome at certain corporations. We have to step into those environments as our true selves and make the change. We need to be mindful of the fact that performance capital is not enough, just doing the job will not be sufficient; as professionals of color, we need to build effective relationships across differences to be truly successful. But we also need to be willing to stay in the fight. Because when we're audacious enough to look like and sound like and BE ourselves, we empower others to be themselves, too.

Sharon: Reba, how does the C-suite at U.S. Bank support this? What is leadership doing to ensure all employees feel valued and accepted?

Reba: Our CEO and Managing Committee at U.S. Bank are fully committed to diversity, equity, and inclusion. Greg and I meet with them regularly and can attest to their deep engagement, willingness to listen and to learn. Each Managing Committee member serves as the lead sponsor for our Business Resource Groups: Alumni, African American, Asian Heritage, Disability, Native American, Nosotros Latinos, Proud to Serve (military), Spectrum LGBTQ, and U.S. Bank Women.

One of the most important ways leadership demonstrates their commitment is by giving their time to travel across our footprint to participate in events with employees. Recently, we hosted summits for our African American and Hispanic employees, and every member of the Managing Committee participated in a significant way. They also participated in training events across the country focused on learning about bias and microaggressions, often hosting listening sessions to hear directly from employees. When our employees see and connect with our Managing Committee, they understand that their commitment is real.

Sharon: Greg, how do you work with leaders and executives to help them change mindsets around inclusion?

Greg: It takes training and lots of honest conversations. I usually start by asking leaders, "Why is this important to you? And don't give me the company answer. I want to know why this is *personally* important to you. **What journey are you willing to go on in order to understand employees who look and act differently from you?** How will you strive to see the best in them?" We spend a lot of time having courageous conversations around how to embrace inclusivity within workspaces, and how to create safe spaces for employees to talk about their experiences, needs, and choices. I work with leaders on giving their direct reports the space they need to express themselves, and creating the right conditions for them to feel confident and comfortable.

It all starts at the top, with the CEO and board of directors, because that's where the tone is set. They've got to be willing to accept that different worldviews exist and have value, and see that surrounding themselves with people who hold those same worldviews is damaging. When I stepped into my role at U.S. Bank, it was in a company with a strong will to change. It doesn't mean we're perfect; we still have a ton of work to do. But I know that an organizational leader must have a deep personal commitment to inclusion work, and at U.S. Bank we're fortunate to have that type of leadership.

Sharon: Over to you, Reba. What's a clear signal that an executive or leader is genuinely committed to building a culture of inclusion?

Reba: I know genuine commitment when I see a couple of signs:

The first one is commitment to learning and growth. Leaders who are focused on continuous improvement, who are willing to learn and grow through experience, are the most likely to commit to take the journey to inclusion.

Another is discomfort. When a leader says, "I did not know" or "I just did not understand," that is where discovery can begin. This usually shows up as discomfort. Most executives achieve high levels of success based on what they know, so it takes courage to acknowledge that there are areas where you may not know and may need help to do better.

The last one is curiosity replacing judgement. Executives are prized for their abilities to quickly evaluate opportunities and prioritize solutions. I know commitment to inclusion when the natural bias towards judgement is replaced by curiosity: "Tell me more about that," or "help me understand." When the executive is talking less and listening more.

Sharon: What would you say to executives who've hired professionals of color for non-leadership roles, but who want to either promote them or simply help them be more effective? How do they spark change within their organizations that will eventually catalyze diverse leadership teams? Greg, what's your take?

Greg: If you think about it, all companies have diversity. Diversity is just dimensions of difference, and all companies have that because they can't possibly hire employees who are all the same in every way. So, **what's truly important to leaders is inclusion. Inclusion is the verb; it's the action of ensuring that everyone on your team is trusted and empowered to contribute at their highest level.** In order to do that, leaders have to understand that there are hurdles and systematic biases that keep certain employees from reaching their full potential.

There's also a huge amount of impetus around equity, and ensuring that we close gaps and disparities in society and within corporations. When I think about equity, I think about creating equal access to opportunity so all people can be at their full potential. That's what a leader's primary job should be. That can mean creating customized development plans that meet individuals where they're at, since all employees aren't starting from the same place. There are disparities and advantages, and leaders must see this and adjust their tactics accordingly. How can you lift up employees who have been left out, overlooked, disproportionately disadvantaged? How can you create opportunities for them, especially leadership opportunities?

Inclusive leadership means digging into your organization, understanding that not all people have the same starting point, and adjusting to provide different support to different people.

Sharon: Authenticity is so important to Greg's work. Reba, what would you say is the number one thing companies should do to prove to professionals of color that their authentic selves are ALWAYS welcome at work?

Reba: Creating a culture of true inclusivity is key. And culture is created by and sustained by people, so one of the most important ways that leaders can encourage professionals of color to bring their authentic selves to work is by being authentic themselves. It is important for our young people to know that you can be authentic and be a successful executive.

I was once told by a boss that I was "too nice" to be successful in business. This feedback was hard to process. My strongest personal belief is the power of kindness. For me, being kind is about treating every human being with the respect they deserve, one of my core values. After receiving this feedback, I contemplated changing my beliefs and approach. Instead, I chose to make it my personal mission to demonstrate that kindness is a leadership strength, not a weakness. You can be kind and achieve results. You can be kind and be tough. You can be kind and disagree. Kindness begets empathy, which is essential to meaningful discourse and forward progress.

Authentic leaders demonstrate and set an example for others. I hope when other young professionals of color see me bringing my whole self to work and being successful in my job, it will inspire them to do the same.

CHAPTER 4

Yes, You CAN Build
a Culture of Inclusion

They came. They saw. They left.

Employee retention is a widespread organizational challenge that's becoming increasingly expensive to combat. And, when it comes to talent of color, **many companies absolutely nail recruitment and hiring, but fail miserably at convincing their new hires to stick around.**

Sound familiar? Maybe your organization has spent decades attempting to build a more diverse workforce and is great at bringing talented employees of color into the fold . . . but few stay longer than a year or two. Perhaps you're starting to get feedback from both employees and applicants of color that your company isn't a good "culture fit." You might even hear similar stories from your colleagues in leadership positions across the region. Even top companies with stellar benefits, advancement opportunities, and great reputations are hemorrhaging their talent of color. And they just don't know why.

But I do.

A great job isn't enough

Many corporate leaders assume that the root of the problem is salaries, promotions, or something concrete, but it's actually much more ephemeral. Professionals of color don't just want job security and overflowing bank accounts; they want to feel like they are truly welcome, safe, and free to be themselves in their workplaces. They want cultural connectivity, a sense of belonging, and the assurance that their professional growth is important to their colleagues and supervisors. They want to be part of a working community, not just a workplace.

If that sounds touchy-feely to you, consider this:

What if you worked in an office where each of your bosses, all the way up to the CEO, looked differently from you and had wildly different life experiences. Let's say 90 percent of your coworkers also grew up in different cultures, listened to different music, or blankly stared when you tried to strike up a conversation about your favorite TV show. Now imagine sitting in a meeting with these folks. Even if you had THE BEST ideas on the planet, would you be eager to raise your voice? Would you feel comfortable sharing your creativity with a population that was, at best, cordial and respectful of you but did nothing to make you feel like part of the team?

Maybe you can honestly say *you* would. But most people wouldn't.

Many leaders think that being a talented and skilled employee who shoulders an engaging workload should be satisfying and sufficient. Interesting work is important, but it's not enough.

Many also believe that all employees are motivated by simple things like money and advancement opportunities. Raises and promotions are important, but they're not enough. *(Side note: Millions of employees are more interested in feeling impactful, relevant, or included than getting paycheck bumps.[13] Just saying.)*

Many of these same leaders are perfectly willing to shell out for "team-building" retreats when the sales department is lagging behind but think "creating a culture of inclusion" for employees of color is a bridge

---

13 Llopis, Glenn. "The Top 9 Things That Ultimately Motivate Employees to Achieve." Forbes. Forbes Magazine, July 16, 2012. https://www.forbes.com/sites/glennllopis/2012/06/04/top-9-things-that-ultimately-motivate-employees-to-achieve/#6390bbae257e.

too far. And that's why they scratch their heads as talent of color flees the company in droves.

Work is never just work. Good jobs include tasks that feel important, recognition and rewards, but also camaraderie, friendships, social connections, and teamwork. **Very few people will thrive if they feel isolated or misunderstood at work. And many, MANY professionals of color feel that way every day.**

Luckily, any company with the will to make its culture more inclusive and welcoming can do it. It'll take some time, some training, and some resources, but the end result will be retaining those fantastic employees of color instead of watching them slip away.

Start by getting the leadership team on board

If you're going to create a shift in company culture, it must start at the top. Your efforts to build and encourage a sense of belonging in your workplace will fall flat unless the work begins at the leadership level. Company founders, the executive team, and key middle managers need to understand the importance of an inclusive work culture and believe in its power.

Even if your leadership team appears to be on board, **it can be helpful to offer them some professional development opportunities around building a welcoming workplace culture.** Pharmaceutical firm Merck & Co. requires *all supervisors* to undergo training in unconscious bias, a behavior that surfaces when individuals judge others based on gender, race, age, or other identity markers without realizing they're doing it. The training helps leaders at Merck become aware of this type of bias and see the value of modeling inclusive behavior. They learn the importance of engaging in active listening and encouraging different points of view, tactics that foster inclusion during meetings, annual reviews, and informal workplace interactions.[14]

It's vital to be vocal about the goals for your company's culture, and that means drafting a clear purpose statement declaring your commitment to cultivating inclusion. Once it's written and approved, spread it around in email newsletters, on your website, in job descriptions and recruitment materials, and at all-hands meetings. In a *Forbes* article, Cat Graham, an HR and culture consultant, offers this recommendation: "Include FAQs to engage everyone with the purpose and how it benefits them individually, as team members and as an organization. Use graphics to show what an inclusive culture looks like at your organization."[15]

---

14 Gurchiek, Kathy. "6 Steps for Building an Inclusive Workplace." Society for Human Resource Management, August 16, 2019. https://www.shrm.org/hr-today/news/hr-magazine/0418/pages/6-steps-for-building-an-inclusive-workplace.aspx.

15 Graham, Cat. "Council Post: Five Strategies To Create A Culture Of Inclusion." Forbes, June 20, 2018. https://www.forbes.com/sites/forbeshumanresourcescouncil/2018/06/20/five-strategies-to-create-a-culture-of-inclusion/#1db9f981c962.

Then, recognize that education and statement-making are just the start. To ensure this cultural shift takes root, you need to create accountability. **How will you make sure managers, supervisors, and execs of all stripes are actually *living out* your inclusion goals?** Will you have quarterly check-ins? Ask each leader to create an inclusion to-do list? Generate an employee survey to see how changes are taking hold and ask each leader to review the results? It's imperative to make a follow-up plan to ensure the shifts become permanent.

Create internal groups and structures to support inclusion

For your next inclusion-building task, make sure employees who currently feel isolated or disconnected have resources. Create safe spaces for them to both express their concerns AND connect with other employees in similar situations. Here are three resources you can create within your company:

> **Employee Resource Groups (ERGs):** An ERG is an employer-recognized group of individuals who share the concerns of a common race, gender identity, national origin, sexual orientation, or other identity markers. Some organizations use different names for this type of group—business resource group, employee network, team member network—but they all serve the same purpose. ERGs can help marginalized or isolated employees connect and channel their energy into efforts that

support business objectives, engagement, and professional development.

Diversity Best Practices reports, "In the past 10 to 15 years, employee resource groups began to prove that they were also business assets by demonstrating their value in recruitment and retention, marketing, brand enhancement, training, and employee development."[16] So, not only will these groups encourage a culture of inclusion, they'll help your company grow stronger in other ways!

Want your talent of color to stick around? Create an ERG for them, support it, and encourage its members to offer feedback and suggestions to your leadership team.

Inclusion Councils: While ERGs create safe spaces for employee-to-employee discussion, it is also helpful to have a layer of mid-level leadership active in inclusion efforts. An Inclusion Council can serve this purpose. This is a small, dedicated group of influential leaders—people who work a level or two below the CEO—tasked with setting goals around hiring, retaining, and advancing a diverse workforce, along with addressing any engagement problems among marginalized groups. The council exists as an advocacy body, a champion of inclusiveness that can funnel concerns from the frontline to the C-suite. Many councils meet quarterly to discuss employee

---

16 "Employee Resource Groups." Diversity Best Practices, March 6, 2018. https://www.diversitybestpractices.com/employee-resource-groups.

concerns, troubleshoot, and relay messages to senior leadership about ideas or problems that have surfaced from the workforce. Every company needs a safe space for tough conversations about diversity; Inclusion Councils can help create that space.

Since employees of color may feel disconnected and disenfranchised, they are not the ones who should be charged with spearheading organizational culture changes. An Inclusion Council composed of diverse, passionate leaders have the power to influence change and take up the charge.

Interest-based lunch/social groups: ERGs and Inclusion Councils are effective because they involve building formalized, official groups where professionals of color can gather and connect. However, your efforts can be augmented with more casual opportunities for connection. By creating lunchtime groups around hobbies or interests, employees are given a fantastic opportunity to meet and connect with coworkers who share similar interests, regardless of race, gender, or ethnicity. Knitters, comic book fans, and budding chefs can gather monthly over lunch to chat about their passions. Book clubs are also a great way to cultivate connectivity, and you can take it a step further by including readings by authors of color for a new way to spark meaningful conversations that help build cultural sensitivity and awareness. If your company is large or decentralized, ask officers or regional leaders to take charge of spreading the word about social groups.

While declaring a company-wide commitment to inclusion sets the tone, professionals of color need more than just rhetoric. Groups like these can be crucial in creating a culturally inclusive environment that helps people stay connected.

Leading Out Loud Principle:
Be a sponsor of inclusion

That's right, there's *even more* you can do to create a working environment that makes talent of color feel valued, seen, and welcome. If you truly want to Lead Out Loud on this issue and retain your diverse employee base, you need to position yourself as a sponsor of inclusion.

Create mentorship opportunities for talent of color:
Even if you're not a person of color yourself, offering formal guidance and mentorship to employees of color can have a huge impact. Feeling connected to other employees with similar life-experiences is essential, but backing that up with a personalized development program, like mentorship, adds another layer of inclusion. By doing this, you send a direct message that not only are you serious about wanting your talent of color to succeed, you are willing to give them the inside scoop on how to accomplish their professional goals. And don't just do this yourself! Encourage other leaders to follow your example.

Organize events specific to professionals of color:
Does your company have a Father's Day celebration or training opportunities specific to emerging female leaders? If you are already organizing gender-specific groups, why not champion

similar events for your diverse employees? Managers and executives should sponsor leadership development events, networking opportunities, and celebrations specific to employees of color so those employees feel engaged and valued.

Push for a Diversity & Inclusion Leader: If your company already has such a role, kudos! You are ahead of the pack. If not, you could be the person who advocates to add a DEI specialist to your leadership team. Help your company show authentic commitment to inclusion by creating an executive role.

In previous chapters we explored the challenges of finding and hiring talent of color, but I hope that this chapter has shown you the value of creating a culture that includes them. Diverse professionals must feel welcome from day one . . . *and beyond.* You can't reel candidates in with promises of equity and advancement, and then leave them feeling excluded and alone. As we learned in chapter 3, employees who bring their authentic selves to work are more inclined to stay. Make your workplace is one that values authenticity and provides opportunities for professionals of color to connect, express themselves, and make change.

Since the future workforce of America is quickly shifting toward professionals of color, retention of these workers should be a top priority for any organization that wants to remain competitive. Your company CAN make it exciting for their diverse employees to come to work—and make it appealing for them to stay. With some passion, some strategy, and some humility, you'll transform your organization into one that knows how to walk the inclusion talk.

DEI work is all about relationships

At this point in the book, you might be hoping for some sort of rubric or checklist or roadmap for building an inclusive culture. You might have scanned the index to see if there's a cheat-sheet for tough conversations about race, or some concise guide to avoiding offensive language and intercultural faux pas.

But here's the thing: there are no shortcuts. There are no apps or tools that will help you navigate the intricacies of changing your corporate culture, promoting leaders of color, or correcting biased behaviors among your workforce. Because, all those things involve people, and each person is unique. You can't make hard-and-fast rules about people and expect them to apply across the board.

And perhaps more importantly, the real work of DEI is about building relationships with diverse people. To be a catalyst for change among different groups of people, you must be willing to become intimate with all the players. If you want to be a leader who attracts and inspires talent of color, you need to cultivate personal relationships with professionals of color. You need to stop seeing diverse people as "other," as a population apart from yourself. And the only way to do that is to actively and thoughtfully build friendships with people who look different from you, and who have likely had very different life experiences from yours.

If you look back on the contents of this chapter, you'll see it's all about community and connection and relationships. ERGs and Inclusion Councils bring diverse people together to work and learn. Mentorship is, by definition, a personal and intense relationship. Every suggestion I've made hinges on reaching out, listening, and learning from diverse peers and employees. And as you continue reading, you'll find more of the same. While I want to offer concrete action items as often as possible, I also need to be clear that creating an equitable workplace requires improvisation, creativity, and a real willingness to forge new relationships.

DEI work absolutely cannot be done at arm's length, and it cannot be done by following some prescribed list of preapproved steps. It's messy and nuanced and deeply personal. But if you're truly committed to cultivating a culture of inclusion, it's work that you'll find deeply and endlessly rewarding.

Leading Out Loud Interview:
JENNIE CARLSON, Retired Chief Human Resources Officer, U.S. Bank

With more than 25 years of experience at U.S. Bank, including 15 as CHRO, Jennie Carlson had the chance to watch the company grow and evolve. As a gifted human resources leader, she insisted that diversity and inclusion become business imperatives for U.S. Bank, frequently and loudly saying she believed they should be standard practice at all businesses. Jennie wanted her employees to understand and reflect the diverse customers the bank served, so she sought to recruit and hire employees from a variety of communities.

I met Jennie at a United Negro College Fund event more than a decade ago, and we've been fighting the good fight together ever since. I was leading UNCF in Minneapolis at the time and was working hard to build relationships with corporations. Jennie, on the other hand, was with a major corporation and was trying to hire more diverse leaders. Ever since our first meeting, we've been having candid conversations about difficult topics in a way that makes us both better.

Jennie has told me that our friendship helped her discover that, as a first-generation college student from a working-class background, she had much more in common with the average HBCU graduate than she did with the professionals who came from stable, middle-class backgrounds. She learned that the headwinds she'd seen in her life—economic status, student loans, lack of professional networks—are true headwinds. But she also learned that she'd had many tailwinds including a stable, two-parent family that owned a modest and mortgaged home, and parents who were supportive of education even if they didn't necessarily understand it. Together, we've discussed our differences and marveled over our similarities.

Recently, Jennie and I chatted about the importance of building and nurturing a culture of inclusion, and she shared some of the tactics she used to make this possible at the fifth largest bank in the United States.

Sharon: First of all, Jennie I want to thank you for Leading Out Loud, and for just being on this journey with me from the beginning. You've been a strong voice and a force for good in the fight for equity, and I'm so glad to know you.

Jennie: I feel the same way! When we first started this work, you were all in. I think that passion has a lot to do with your upbringing. But regardless, oh my gosh Sharon, thank heaven you showed up. I feel safer taking risks and pushing this agenda because I have you with me. We are a compelling team. We complement each other well, and we've developed a real sense of trust. I am lucky to have you.

Sharon: I'd love for you to talk a little about how you shifted the culture when you were at U.S. Bank. How did inclusion become a priority for you?

Jennie: Well, I used to go to meetings where I was the only woman in the room, and there was absolutely *no one* of color there. This was true more generally in the early days, and then later, as I moved up into the leadership levels of the pyramid, at the top. The further up the pyramid, the more likely women and people of color were either to jump out of the pipeline or get pushed out. White, heterosexual men still dominated the

C-suite in many industries. I wanted to help change that and bring people with different experiences to all levels, including the very top of the pyramid.

Sharon: So how do corporate CEOs get this right? Moving more professionals of color into the C-suite, into management, leading teams. What is holding them back? If we're going to affect culture change from the top down, how do we do that?

Jennie: We have to first acknowledge that CEOs have good intentions. They want to do this. They have spent a lot of money trying to do it. Their hearts are pure. They don't know, however, what they don't know. And, they think they can fix nearly any problem by deciding to work on it. The resolution, in this case, depends on a different way of solving problems. It is not just a work issue, but a cultural and life experience one. CEOs and other C-suite leaders need to think beyond who they work with, and consider *who they spend time with?* Who is in your personal network? As a practical matter, CEOs often have relatively limited personal networks, often made up of people who are very much like them. That's not where the opportunity is. There's a reason we don't have Business Resource Groups for White men. They don't need them. They have the American business environment.

Many people live in places where the other residents tend to look like them. Unless you actively make the effort to socialize outside your home space, you're probably not taking sufficient risk with your personal life. You are less likely to grow beyond where you are in this area. Who do CEOs play golf with?

On their own? At company outings? Is it the same people all the time? Do the executive assistants who set up the foursomes invite people they know the CEO will feel comfortable with? Or, nearly as bad, do they pick people who are most comfortable *asking* to spend time with the CEO, who are comfortable making those requests because they look like the CEO and have similar life experiences? C-suite executives will benefit from breaking out of the protective bubble that their positions enable and interacting with more diverse groups. They are likely to hear things they would not ordinarily hear, and learn about the wide range of different experiences.

CEOs should ask themselves about their friends. Who do you call when you have a problem? Who do you call when you want to celebrate? Who do you call when you want to talk things through? Who can call YOU and say, "I just want to chat."?

As a corporate leader, you risk isolation. You sit with the same people at church, invite the same people to your home, and often those are the people you think of when business opportunities arise. Fundamentally changing as a person is not the goal. Investing time in relationships and even friendships with people who look and have experiences that are different from you is. Both sides will learn and benefit.

The challenge for leaders at the very top of the pyramid is to expand their personal networks, build genuine friendships with people outside of their usual experience zones and forge real empathy and understanding. Otherwise, much of what they try to do on the inclusion front can ring hollow. Talking the talk without walking the walk never works in the long term.

Sharon: Are there any other factors at play that keep C-suite leaders from building friendships with people of color and other marginalized groups?

Jennie: Women and people of color are less likely to view things like going to lunch with their boss or getting coffee with the CEO as business imperatives. Women see those opportunities primarily as social instead of business networking opportunities, and so these interactions become things to do after they've finished everything else. And, if they're trying to get home to be with the kids, it may never happen. People of color often are exhausted by not being authentic at work or are intimidated by the sheer differences in experience and stature. Networking up the pyramid is an important part of your career progression. We need to help people to see this.

Sharon: How did you come to understand all this on a personal level?

Jennie: I learned it very personally through my relationship with you.

Ken Charles, who was at General Mills at the time, was helping us with our DEI efforts at U.S. Bank very early on. This was years and years ago. He said, "We're doing a United Negro College Fund gala and U.S. Bank should get involved." You were working for UNCF at the time. The easy thing for me would have been to delegate and send one of our Black employees to the event and not worry about it. But I thought, "This is a big deal, and I'm going to show up myself." So, we went to a meeting at

General Mills. It was one of the first times in my life I was in a meeting with primarily Black people. And you were there. And we really hit it off.

Sharon: Yeah, we did!

Jennie: And then we had lunch and started doing more things together, and I think our relationship opened both of our eyes. But, I have to say that I'm not sure I would have gone to that General Mills meeting two or three years before that. It was way outside my comfort zone. But I did it, and it made a difference.

When you think about the opportunities CEOs have to show up, and how many times they pass, it's frustrating. I recognize that a busy corporate leader can't do everything, but sometimes you must be more intentional in your choices. You don't have to go to the same galas, community events, and meet-and-greets every year.

Sharon: Exactly. As a leader, if you are committed to diversity, equity, and inclusion, you've got to step out of your comfort zone. So, if you're going to eighteen different galas attended primarily by White people, maybe you can choose one that's a little bit more diverse.

Jennie: No question.

Sharon: Let's talk about what you did at the bank. How did you ensure that professionals of color felt supported and nurtured? How did you make sure they felt welcome and valued so they wouldn't leave? How did you create a culture where talent of color felt like they belonged?

Jennie: If you're going to create a culture of inclusion, you have to think about the things that happen automatically for others, for the majority, and make them happen for everyone. You have to say: "When I walk down the hall, I'm going to walk down the hall to see *you*, as well as everybody who looks like me." You have to be mindful of treating people equitably, all day every day.

People who went to the same school as half the organization have an automatic "in." People who trained at Historically Black Colleges or Universities, or perhaps a cheaper, less prestigious school, *do not*. As a leader, you need to say: "We're going to surround these people with resources. We're going to connect them with others who feel isolated so they can share ideas and feel more connected within the company."

Create mentoring opportunities, both formal and informal. Employees of color are more likely to advance if a leader is looking out for them, someone who says, "You can miss this meeting, but you sure can't miss *that* one. You can be late for your face-to-face with this guy, but not for *that* guy." Share all the secret codes, all the secret handshakes, and be overt and intentional about it. Because we've all grown up in different cultures where we pick up different cues, so you've got to say: "These are the cues that are important in corporate America. Watch for them."

Sharon: How do we get people of color moved into positions of leadership faster?

Jennie: The best way to do it is to have more people of color at the top. The more people of color you have in leadership roles, the more others will see that applying for those roles is a possibility. To get that first group situated, take more risks. Appoint people, promote people, move them up in the ranks even if they're still a little green. You can't do it the way you've always done it and expect the results to be different.

Studies show that White men are often promoted on the basis of potential, while women are promoted based on actual results. Look at the potential all around, and recognize that potential may look different from what it has traditionally looked like.

Also, make sure not to throw someone into the ocean alone; include enough support for them to be successful in a leadership role. Everybody wants to grow from within. So, you've got to say to yourself, "What signals is our workplace sending about what you have to do to be at the top?"

Sharon: In terms of support mechanisms, would you say ERGs or Inclusion Councils are more important? What has worked best at U.S. Bank?

Jennie: ERGs or Inclusion Councils are important because they provide a safe place for people outside of the traditional corporate pipeline to compare notes, share tactics, and support each other. They are important to creating a sense of belonging that is key to retention and engagement.

Sharon: Can you share a success story of a professional of color at U.S. Bank?

Jennie: We recruited a very senior African American woman. She'd grown up in Alabama, was brilliant, and had spent a number of years at McKinsey & Company before ending up at Wells Fargo. She came to U.S. Bank and to Minnesota, and looked around meetings and said out loud, "Where are all of the Black people?" She was courageous and incredibly qualified.

We had an offsite strategy meeting for the top 200 executives of over 73,000 employees. At the meet-and-greet cocktail hour, one of the senior regional leaders asked her where she was from. She said, "Minnesota. I live in Minnesota." He said, "No, I mean what country are you from?" And she said, "The United States." He said, "No, I mean, what is your country of origin?" He simply could not comprehend that a smart, accomplished Black woman could have grown up in Alabama and ended up in a very senior position at U.S. Bank.

This gifted, powerful woman shared this anecdote with me, and I shared it with our CEO. A year or two previously, he might've replied, "Oh, that's how just so-and-so is. He doesn't mean anything by it," and brushed off the whole incident. But instead, we talked about it at the managing committee meeting. And, as part of the follow-up to that offsite strategy meeting, we spoke to everyone about how it felt to be part of the majority and asked them to consider how it might feel to be part of the minority. After that, many leaders across divisions apologized personally to our African American colleague and began to heal the rift. It was an awkward and painful situation, but it led to some important clarity.

The bottom line is that company culture matters and, in the best companies, that culture is everywhere. The best way to move a culture forward from everywhere is to have it be modeled at the top and consistent all the way through. For many years the corporate CEO—a middle-aged, White, heterosexual, tall man—was the culture carrier. Former U.S. Bank CEO Richard Davis, who wrote the introduction for this book, prepared for his retirement by helping me become the culture carrier for our company. Since I'm a White woman, that represented a small step forward in the diversity and inclusion realm but was still not where we needed to be. Within a year or so, the culture carriers of the company had become an Indian woman and an African American man (Greg Cunningham, from the interview in chapter 3), both of whom have earned tremendous respect from within the company and in our shared communities. They know that their job is to carry that culture of U.S. Bank forward.

CHAPTER 5

Diverse Leaders Inspire Diverse Employees

There's an old maxim, "If you can't see it, you can't be it," that is appropriate for this part of our journey. We saw an excellent example of how it plays out in real life through the stories of Katherine Johnson, Dorothy Vaughan, and Mary Jackson, the three African American women who were featured in the 2016 film, *Hidden Figures*, which told the story of their instrumental roles that helped NASA put astronaut John Glenn into orbit and win the Space Race.

The book and the film depict their inspirational stories, beset by a time in history when much of the country was still battling racial segregation and gender inequality. These remarkable women defied the odds and excelled in mathematical, engineering, and leadership roles traditionally dominated by White men.

But the team making the film wanted to do more than tell these stories.

It's unusual to see Black actors cast as scientists, and even more unusual to see Black women in roles that revolve around math and science. Seeing an opportunity to expand young minds, the *Hidden Figures* cast sponsored free screenings of the movie in Virginia, Georgia, Illinois, Texas, Washington, D.C., Houston, Chicago, and Atlanta the month after it was released.[17] Other organizations followed suit, and soon the film was being shown to eager middle school and high school audiences across the country.

And you know what? It had a huge impact. Much has been written about the waves made by this groundbreaking film. In dozens of articles, African American girls and young women tell reporters they had never imagined they could become rocket scientists or astronauts or high-level mathematicians because they'd

17   Muller, Marissa G. "Hidden Figures Is Already Inspiring Women to Seek Careers in Science and Tech." Glamour. Glamour, January 31, 2017. https://www.glamour.com/story/hidden-figures-inspiring-young-women-science-and-technology.

never been exposed to any examples. They had never seen or read about or even *heard* about African American women tackling jobs in hard science, so they just assumed that those jobs weren't "for" them. Watching *Hidden Figures* changed their minds. They set new goals, joined STEM groups at their schools, entered science fairs, reimagined their futures. Seeing Black women be scientists showed them *they could also be scientists*.

Can your employees envision themselves in the C-suite?

Simplistic as it sounds, we base our beliefs about ourselves (and people like us) on the examples we see in our lives. If we've never seen a man do ballet, we may assume men just don't do ballet. If we've never seen a Latinx professor, we may assume Latinx people can't be professors. If we've never seen someone who looks like us become successful or powerful in the ways we dream of, we may believe our dreams are unreasonable. Outlandish. Impossible.

The overarching theme here is that representation matters. And, although that phrase may have worn out its welcome on some corporate campuses, I'm going to risk repeating it here. **Representation DOES matter. It matters because the examples we see shape our ideas of who we can become.** It matters because many companies claim to want leaders of color, but then they can't understand why none of their employees of color apply for major promotions. It matters because fostering a diverse and equitable workplace involves showing the entire company that talented, driven people from marginalized groups can rise to the C-suite.

So, who's in your C-suite now? Who's on your corporate board? Who gives keynotes at the conferences your organization hosts, and who leads all-hands meetings? Who gets awards and promotions and feature stories in the company newsletter? Hiring talent of color is a vitally important step in the right direction. Nurturing a company culture that celebrates inclusion gets you even farther down the right path, but **until you've got employees of color in visible, influential leadership roles, there's work yet to be done.**

Start with the board

I've worked with hundreds of leaders at dozens of companies over the course of my career, and most of them agree that infusing a leadership team with talent of color works best when it starts at the corporate board level.

This is not news.

For many years now, research has proven that diverse boards perform better. A recent study by McKinsey & Company found that organizations with mixed gender boards were 21 percent more likely to outperform on profitability compared with their peers, and companies that incorporated ethnic and cultural diversity at this level were 33 percent more likely to lead in profitability within their industries.[18] An independent study by researchers at Utah State University concluded that companies with a higher level of racial diversity in the boardroom catalyzed more breakthrough improvements in products and created stronger governance mechanisms.[19] The evidence is clear: diverse boards are strong, effective, and desirable.

Make-A-Wish CEO Richard Davis—whom you met in the foreword—also points out that boards are influential across leadership levels. Diverse boards give people with marginalized perspectives the chance to impact how corporations are run.

"The board needs to be comprised of people of color before management teams will understand the importance of inclusion," Richard explains. "Board diversity is crucially important because board members will inspire through their own behaviors, experiences, and actions. They will share those experiences with the CEO, who will listen and be affected by their perspectives and input. The board comes first. Management comes second because the board dictates what matters to the CEO. The CEO responds most directly to the board

18 Wardell, Lisa. "Board Diversity Propels Performance." Corporate Board Member, March 26, 2018. https://boardmember.com/board-diversity-propels-performance/.

19 Cook, Alison, and Christy Glass. "Do Minority Leaders Affect Corporate Practice? Analyzing the Effect of Leadership Composition on Governance and Product Development." SAGE Journals, December 17, 2014. https://journals.sagepub.com/doi/abs/10.1177/1476127014564109.

because that group of people is, essentially, their only boss."

But what about the impact of board makeup on company *culture*? If you're determined to build an organization that values inclusion from top to bottom, inside and out, focusing on fiscal reasons won't work. That whip-smart mid-level manager who's been with the company for eighteen months won't care as much about the company's bottom-line as he will about his own advancement prospects. (And rightly so.) If your corporate board shows him that talent of color rise to the top, he's more likely to stick around. Professionals of color are more loyal to companies that hire and promote diverse leaders.

So, start with the board. Make sure that its members reflect the racial, ethnic, gender, orientation, age, and experience diversity you want to see in the rest of your company. That may mean appointing some folks who aren't already CEOs, or who are relatively new to board membership. It may mean stepping outside your comfort zone. But, as we've already established, you can't keep doing the same things and expect different results. Take some risks. Bring in some fresh blood. And watch as your diverse board inspires loyalty, action, and ambition at all levels of your company.

Encourage talent of color to pursue leadership roles

Do you have an opening for a VP or division head? Are you recruiting for a CTO or director of marketing? If you want professionals of color to know you're eager for them to apply, you need to say so. And I don't mean including the boilerplate "Equal Opportunity Employer" language on your job postings. Recruitment for managerial and leadership roles should emphasize openness to diverse applicants in multiple ways.

HOW: Use language that is inclusive, welcoming, and specific. Don't just say "open to diverse candidates." Try something like: "Since our company thrives on innovation that's driven by a wide variety of perspectives, we're especially excited to interview candidates of color, candidates who identify as women, and Millennial or Gen Z candidates." Talk to those groups you want to apply, and connect that desire back to organizational values when you can.

WHERE: If you're recruiting internally, don't just post leadership job openings to the company intranet and leave it at that. Seek out spaces and groups that attract employees of color. Naturally, you'll want to connect with any ERGs or diversity councils to help spread the word, but also consider working with departments and teams that are staffed by talent of color. Make sure the opening, job description, and deadlines are posted or distributed.

And, when you're recruiting externally, refer back to the advice shared in chapter 2: in addition to posting on Indeed and Glassdoor, also post on Jopwell and DiversityJobs.com, and become an Equity Hiring and Advancement Partner with People Of Color Careers™. Sponsor booths at job fairs hosted by

Historically Black Colleges and Universities (HBCUs); partner with the highly popular People Of Color Career Fair; make your leadership opening visible in spaces that are frequented by professionals of color.

WHEN: Often! Make sure that leadership positions are discussed across the company on a regular basis. Ask execs and managers to announce any openings at gatherings and discuss them with their employees of color at one-on-one meetings. As often as you can, repeat that you hope to fill this position with a candidate of color (without sounding like a broken record, that is). It takes bravery to apply for promotions, and hearing multiple times that applications from candidates of color are eagerly anticipated may help some amazing employees overcome their initial hesitations.

WHY: Finally, explain WHY having the perspective of a professional of color will be beneficial to each specific position. Is it because this leader will be working with other marginalized groups? Is it because a large portion of your customers are people of color? Is it because the position leads a team that thrives on the dynamic created by a diverse set of experiences? Yes, you want leaders of color because they support a robust company culture . . . but candidates need to hear more. Don't talk about leadership in general terms, focus on the unique role. Why will a leader of color thrive within your company, and how will your company thrive under their direction and leadership?

Support and promote promising leaders of color

If you're panicking a little because you have enough trouble filling *non-leadership roles* with diverse candidates, I'd encourage you to rewind back to chapter 2 for a little review. There are untold numbers of qualified, eager, talented, innovative applicants of color out there, and I've given you several proven strategies for reaching and inspiring them!

However, let's throw another one on the fire: promising leaders of color *within the company* must be supported and nurtured by current executives.

Make sure your entire leadership team knows that professionals of color who show an interest in, or a knack for, leadership should be encouraged. That may mean recommending them for mentorship programs, suggesting they lead certain projects, offering to send them to classes or professional development trainings, or praising them publicly for taking initiative. It's fine to let the individual supervisor make the call, but it can be helpful to provide a list of concrete ways to support budding leaders of color.

In some cases, this may also mean moving professionals of color from the bottom to the top. If the candidates who are applying externally aren't the right fit for a particular leadership role, then take a leap of faith and appoint them or develop them internally. In many cases, someone who is already familiar with your company's culture, politics, niche, industry, and structure will be better suited to leading teams within that company. Executives must decide who their emerging leaders are, and then provide them with the professional support they need to become successful.

Once more with feeling: representation matters! If your organization waxes poetic about the importance of diversity but has a C-suite stacked with White males, your claims will ring false. We all want proof that people who look like us can succeed, and for professionals of color that means seeing diverse leaders.

Leading Out Loud Principle:

Make diverse leadership a priority

Ensuring that professionals of color move into leadership roles within your organization is essential. But as a leader yourself, there are policies you can create, actions you can take, and decisions you can make to further illustrate how important it is to build a diverse leadership team. Here are three key ways you, as a leader, can show professionals of color that they have a bright future at your organization:

Set and execute diversity goals: Don't just talk—DO. If your company insists that its executives create and execute on diversity goals at all leadership levels, that proves to current and prospective employees that you are truly committed. And then, when goals are met, spread the word! Celebrate! Make sure your entire organization knows you are following through on your promise to hire, support, and promote employees of color.

Tie DEI goals to executive compensation: Yep, I know that's a scary one. But again, it sends a crystal-clear message to everyone, inside and outside of your organization, that you're not just blowing smoke. When leaders know that they have the potential to earn more if they hire more talent of color or promote diverse candidates into visible roles, they'll work harder to do so. Simple as that.

Ensure that diverse leaders are in the spotlight: We're circling back to "if you can't see it, you can't be it" again. Once you've got some stellar leaders of color in place, talk about them. Highlight their accomplishments. Praise their progress. Diverse leaders should be visible both internally (newsletters, all-hands) and externally (websites, marketing materials). Because the more other employees of color see them, the easier it will be for them to imagine themselves in similar roles.

It's so easy to claim that "diverse leadership" is a priority at your company, but it's much more challenging to prove that you are taking real steps toward making a diverse executive team a reality. There's nothing more irritating to a talented professional of color than an organization that fails to deliver on its diversity promises. So, do what you can, as an individual leader, to influence policies and catalyze changes that show everyone how serious you are about bringing talent of color into YOUR organization's C-suite.

Leading Out Loud Interview:

DR. REATHA CLARK KING, former Vice President, General Mills Corporation and former President, Executive Director, and Chairman of the Board of Trustees, General Mills Foundation

It's no exaggeration to say that Dr. Reatha Clark King is a legend. This trailblazing woman has fought many hard battles throughout her life, and never doubted her value and worth. She spent her childhood years working in the cotton fields and on her aunt's farm in Georgia. She then went on to graduate from Moultrie High School for Negro Youth in 1954 as valedictorian of her class. She had planned to become a home economics teacher, but an introductory chemistry class changed that. Reatha realized she was wired for science and went on to earn a doctorate in physical chemistry from University of Chicago.

But wait! There's more! Reatha studied a chemical reaction called fluoride flame calorimetry, and her findings made it possible to build the engine that powered Apollo 11, the NASA craft that landed on the moon in 1969. She had a long career as a chemistry professor, then as president of a Minnesota university, before deciding to try her hand at business. In 1988, Reatha was hired to serve as vice president of the General Mills Corporation AND president and executive director of the General Mills Foundation simultaneously. She stayed with the company until 2003, after which she dedicated herself to serving on corporate and nonprofit boards, advising educational councils and further adding to her record of generous philanthropy.

Make no mistake, Reatha Clark King is out to make the world a better, smarter, more equitable place. Single-handedly, if necessary.

Since Reatha has sat on the boards of ExxonMobil, Wells Fargo & Company, Department 56; Minnesota Mutual Companies, and the H. B. Fuller Company, I knew she'd be the perfect person to speak with about the importance of boards in corporate diversity, equity, and inclusion efforts. I was honored to sit down with her and soak up her wisdom!

Sharon: Reatha, I wanted to talk to you today because of your breadth of experience. I believe that many corporate leaders—our CEOs, CHROs, COOs, and others—are missing out on an opportunity by not taking the time to really diversify their boards. Since you have so much experience on corporate boards, I was hoping you'd give us the benefit of that experience. Can you tell us about the boards that you've been on, but also why it's imperative that CEOs and leaders do a better job at making sure that they're more racially inclusive on their boards?

Reatha: Yes, I'd be delighted to comment on that!

First, we want CEOs and heads of companies to accept diversity as a value. You've got to value it and accept that you will not fully benefit from diversity just by assembling a mixed group. Sometimes a group of board members may appear diverse but offer very similar ideas and contributions. Even if the people themselves are diverse, they might not feel comfortable sharing their experiences with the entire board. You're not benefiting from diversity of thought if people don't participate, right? You need to get the person who's carrying that brilliance in their head to feel engaged. You need to allow *diversity of thought* to thrive.

Leaders are responsible for shaping the culture so people can feel relaxed and free to be candid. I call that building a culture for candor, a space where everyone can speak out and give you their honest opinion and not feel that they're going to be penalized.

So, an important shift is going from having a mixed group—where you have the numbers and the diversity quotas filled—to getting into people's heads and benefiting from that diversity of thought. You make your organization smarter when you do this because that diversity of thought will lead to new ideas—ideas for problem solving, ideas for innovation that you wouldn't have had access to if everyone in the room looked and thought in the same way. That's the first step—valuing diversity on boards because it leads to diversity of thought.

Then, you've got to move to that stage of inclusiveness where board members are working together and benefitting from each other's knowledge. That's where human resource officers become so valuable.

Sharon: Which of the boards you've served on worked best, and why? Which ones moved the needle forward on diversity, equity, and inclusion?

Reatha: The ones that built diversity into the company, from hiring on out. The ones that started early by recruiting the smartest people out of Historically Black Colleges and Universities. Brilliance doesn't end at Stanford and Yale. If you leave out Spelman and Morehouse, you're missing out on a chance to make your company smarter.

I also saw good work being done by the boards that engaged executives at all levels. Middle managers and supervisors see things the CEO just won't see. The CEO might go around thinking, oh, everything's fine . . . but he or she is not engaging and tapping into the heads of middle managers. The diversity of a mixed group is essential, but so is knowing the reality of people's experiences. Otherwise it's just optics, a board that looks good but isn't effective.

Sharon: As a leader of color, how did you influence choices and policies on corporate and nonprofit boards?

Reatha: As a Black leader, you want to develop yourself into being a role model. As an executive within a company, you want to get to a place where you can have a voice on diversity. You want to be able to speak truth to power, and say, "We are not as good as we should be and can be."

When I was chair of the board for the National Association of Corporate Directors, one of the things we focused on was how to define diversity. When you're a global company, you'll be considering factors like racial, gender, and cultural diversity. Do you include all of those and more? In the end, we realize that's for every board to think about and to define for themselves. But if they don't, if they don't talk about what diversity means within their own company, they'll struggle.

I've also encouraged corporate leaders to listen to their employees when it comes to making diversity a priority. I sat on the board for a financial services company, and the human resources officer brought me a copy of the annual employee satisfaction survey. I shared it with the board and was very open about the feedback that we were getting from employees. I asked the board members the question, "How do you think the employees said we did around the racial diversity expectation?" And, "Have you gone to the employees to ask how they would address racial inequity in our company?"

Sharon: But don't you think the CEO has to set the tone, Reatha, and make the hard decisions?

Reatha: Absolutely.

Sharon: It's the leaders who need to say, "This is the kind of company we're going to have."

Reatha: Yes, definitely. The leadership must set the tone, and boards have a number of ways and opportunities to engage with the CEO around this. The board is basically an oversight group that works to make the company as good as it can possibly be. We do this through contributing ideas, asking questions, but also by critiquing the aspirations and standards set by the CEO. If the CEO is not setting any aspirations, I think you're in trouble.

Sharon: What advice would you give to professionals of color who would like to join corporate boards? What are the steps they need to take?

Reatha: When I mentor young board members, people aspiring to be on boards, they ask me, "What should I be working on?" I tell them, number one, learn what is involved in board governance. They need to understand that is different from managing the company, and that they'll need to learn to analyze problems in a rigorous way. Before you try to join a board, you need to know what board service entails.

On the flip side of that, I tell them don't fear that you are too green. Yes, some board members will have decades of experience, but they bring different things to the table. Certainly do your homework on the board materials and the company itself, but don't let your newness hold you back.

Then, I tell them to remember that the board is an oversight group and to let the CEO and executives run the company. Don't come in micromanaging. There is a place, a time when you can ask for all the details you want, but that place and time is not a board meeting.

Finally, I tell them to participate. You learn by participating. If you come to a meeting and just sit quiet and don't ask questions, don't participate, don't make suggestions, then you are missing an opportunity. Join a board to be a part of it, not to observe it.

CHAPTER 6

How to Lead Out Loud

As I've said in earlier chapters, I cannot provide you with a checklist or a roadmap for transforming your own company from the inside out. I cannot whip up a concise guide to difficult conversations or tell you how to steer clear of race- or diversity-related landmines. I can only ask that you embrace the nuanced, complex world of DEI work as it is instead of trying to put hard, universal parameters around it. The reason I can't provide a fool-proof formula is because Leading Out Loud on diversity, equity, and inclusion will look different for each individual leader. And because Leading Out Loud is an art, not a science.

James C. Burroughs II, Chief Equity and Inclusion Officer at Children's Minnesota, knows this better than most. He has more than 25 years of experience in non-profit management, diversity and inclusion, and employment law. This amazing man has been my partner in crime to make Minnesota a more diversity-minded region. He was the first ever inclusion officer for the State of Minnesota, he partnered with me during the early days of the People of Color Career Fairs in our region, and we continue to collaborate on new projects, ideas, and initiatives.

Currently, he's the chief equity and inclusion officer for Children's Minnesota, one of the largest freestanding pediatric health systems in the United States. Since he's been such a strong partner and ally to me in this crucial work for multiple decades, I asked him for suggestions for CEOs, executives, and other business leaders who want to build stronger and more authentic relationships with professionals of color.

3 DEI Recommendations from James C. Burroughs II

James believes that leadership actions must be designed to advance equity, diversity, and inclusion, and that those actions should be monitored and measured.

"Leaders learn and perform best when they share their successes and challenges with others and acknowledge what could have been done differently to achieve success," he explains. "So, it's essential to establish performance metrics to measure diversity, equity, and inclusion actions, and share best—and unsuccessful—practices with other companies."

Along the same lines, he points out that DEI strategies should never be treated as isolated, stand-alone initiatives. These strategies must be integrated into the goals and metrics for organizational success and measured regularly in order to establish alignment to overall success. And I couldn't agree more; one of the best ways to encourage follow-through is to track, measure, and report out.

When I asked James why so many leaders shy away from spearheading DEI work, he pointed out that many simply haven't been trained in how to handle these topics.

"Leaders guiding diverse teams must be educated on the principles of inclusive leadership," he said. "Inclusive leadership creates environments where everyone can bring their full selves to work, and also helps create an inclusive space for all employees to be successful. Education will help executive leaders recognize and minimize their blind spots and create inclusive environments to facilitate more open and honest conversations that lead to more inclusive behaviors with better results."

One of our shared frustrations has always been that companies get burned out on DEI work so quickly. A corporation that's willing to pour time, human power, and money into community outreach, internal collaboration, and trainings one year may abandon diversity initiatives entirely the next. James maintains it has to do with planning for the long term—both strategically and financially—and that planning should revolve around helping employees succeed.

"The companies that are truly committed to transformative DEI work are the ones that focus on the design and implementation of DEI professional development for all employees," James told me. "Corporate leaders must intentionally invest in the growth and development of their entire workforce. Retention of employees of color will increase when those employees are given the tools to successfully deliver and perform, while at the same time enhancing their future growth and development."

James and I both believe that leadership in diversity, equity, and inclusion requires bold actions, and that the best leaders focus those actions on ensuring their employees feel safe, valued, and seen. Government, education, business, and nonprofit leaders must make good on the inherent promise that all people should be able to bring their authentic selves to work and unleash their full potential. Because, at the end of the day, companies are comprised of people. If the talented people of color at your company feel like your DEI work is all theory and no practice, all talk and no action, they won't care how much money you pour into it. Your workforce needs to experience your commitment to diversity, equity, and inclusion on a personal level, or it will seem empty and meaningless to them.

In fact, I think it's time we hear from some employees.

Input from working professionals of color

So far, we've put the focus squarely on corporate leaders who have worked hard to create change inside their companies. These bold executives have shared stories of their triumphs and missteps and have offered their advice on the best ways to Lead Out Loud on all things DEI. But now let's look at some constructive input from diverse employees themselves.

Your in-person DEI Dream Team may still be forming, but your virtual team is right here. And they're ready to share their advice and insights. So here we go. Below you'll find a few stories you might hear if you held a roundtable and invited professionals of color to share their experiences directly with you.

Insights from a business development professional of color

ON FILLING QUOTAS AND SAVING FACE: I remember the day I landed my first internship at RBC Dain Rauscher. I was so excited because, unlike most of my peers whose internships came through inroads, my internship came through sheer will and some divine intervention. On my first day, I was given a tour of the department, where I was welcomed by some but not all. **I ended my tour in the office of a V.P., where I vividly**

remember feeling like he didn't care I was sitting there at all. In fact, at one point he turned to the hiring manager and said, "Now we need to hire one woman and one more person of color for quota." I was flabbergasted and befuddled. I then realized right away that these shiny words called "diversity" and "inclusion" were thrown around in corporations for face-value alone. I realized that the company didn't see my talent as an asset. My skin color was what the company saw as an asset. It was for the company's website, pamphlets, and to meet a quota.

ON THE VALUE OF INCLUSION AND PAIN OF TOKENISM: Have you ever felt like the only chocolate chip in the cookie dough? Well, most people of color have had that experience multiple times. I remember aspiring to hold a managerial position at my previous company, where I'd been promoted quickly and ranked among the top three sales reps in the company. I had an associate at the time who also ranked high alongside me. He was a White guy who never spoke about being a manager and had no real ambition or aspirations. However, he was groomed for leadership right away, quietly. I'd see him getting invited to managers-only meetings (which were rooms full of White men), and I wondered why I wasn't in that room.

Being inquisitive, I asked a manager about the meeting; he gave me a nonchalant answer. I asked another manager—a guy with whom I felt I had a good rapport—and his response was, "They didn't tell you about the meeting? You are one of our top reps. You should have been in there." (He'd known they hadn't told me about the meeting. He was just attempting to backpedal.)

I ended up attending the next managers-only meeting so they could save face. I immediately noticed I was the only chocolate chip in the cookie dough. All White men, no women, and no managers of color. At the end of the meeting, a manager walked over and pretended to give me advice, but actually just used nice words to discourage me from pursuing a management role: "You're one our top reps! Managers don't make as much money as you can as a rep. I would stay a rep if I were you."

I had a multitude of different feelings. The two that permeated through my mind and body most were: **None of the current managers looked like me so I had no role model, and I'd never get the support and grooming that my White associates were getting.** After a while, I saw this behavior repeated and my employee cynicism grew; eventually, I left the company.

ADVICE FOR CORPORATE LEADERS: Understand that **you can't have diversity without inclusion.** Companies tend to focus on one piece to fill a quota, and those companies have struggled to retain talent of color because of it. DEI, in my opinion, should be a part of every company's training materials and orientation curriculum.

Insights from a PR and multimedia professional of color

ON LEAVING A DEI LEGACY AND DIVERSE REPRESENTA-TION: I was nine months pregnant when I was terminated from my job at a media company because I wasn't eligible for maternity leave under Federal Medical Leave Act. Shockingly, this was legal, but that doesn't mean that it was the right thing to do.

When I'd been hired for this position eleven months earlier, my direct supervisor had been an advocate for diversity and inclusion who had used her own career to break glass ceilings in our field. However, about two months after she'd hand-selected me to work for her, she retired. The person who'd been her boss didn't have the same values and used her replacement to "clean house." **Less than a year after she retired, all the candidates of color she'd hired had been let go for different reasons. This included me, and although I made many attempts to negotiate for maternity leave instead of termination, I was forced out.** If my original supervisor had been able to lay some groundwork around inclusion, or codify her reasons for hiring diverse candidates, the company may have gone in a different direction.

After spending a few months with my new baby, I moved on, landing a temporary position at a local government agency. What was challenging in this new organization was the culture. Within the agency, there were multiple initiatives, committees, and task forces addressing issues of diversity and inclusion, but all these efforts were being spearheaded by White men and women. Why? And how can a group of White men and women create solutions for communities of color? How can a group of White men and women create programming for communities of color without any input from people of color themselves? More importantly, how can elected officials sit back and let this happen? If we are going to service diverse communities, we need diverse input on how to do so effectively.

ON UNCONSCIOUS BIAS IN HIRING: In between these two jobs, I had applied to four other companies. Government wasn't a great fit for me because my background was in the broadcasting industry. So, to stay in my career field, I applied to every major player in the market. I was told by most of them that I didn't have enough experience.

During a networking event, I met an employee at one of these media companies who was still in college. He was a young White man, and he'd been hired while still in school and quite green. I was curious to know **how that company could justify telling me, a Black woman with ten years of experience and a bachelor's degree that she didn't have enough experience, and then turn around and hire a White man with no experience and no degree.** Think about the message that sends about how we value people. How we view them to be capable and competent, not based on education or experience, but based on the color of their skin.

I wish I could say that this was an isolated incident, but similar situations are happening across the board in all industries. This can't change overnight, and it won't change without your help.

ADVICE FOR CORPORATE LEADERS: As a CEO or executive, you have the power to improve the living conditions and working conditions for an entire workforce. Be brave. We can no longer afford to let executives sit back and keep doing things the way they've always been done. Thousands of professionals of color are leaving companies where leadership is complacent because they see no hope of moving their careers forward. They're pursuing opportunities with organizations that make DEI a priority.

Be in tune with what is happening on the ground. Set a tone inside your organization that allows your leaders to explore nontraditional solutions to retain your employees. Think about how much a person like me could have benefitted if I'd had "discretionary unpaid leave," or how my life would've changed if the HR rep had decided to recognize the loopholes in maternity leave laws and take my case higher up. **When employers provide solutions, it sets a precedent for other companies to follow suit. That chain reaction can influence lawmakers, and that is how you can create societal change.**

Lastly, do not accept all white boards, C-suites, or management teams. If you are okay with them, they will continue. **Set a goal and set a deadline and hold someone responsible. For example, say: "We must have 30 percent of XYZ positions held by people of color by 2025." If you don't create concrete milestones, you will struggle to retain professionals of color** because you will have created a glass ceiling that they can't break through. And you will fail to reach your full revenue potential, because a room full of White people can never tell you how to develop, market, or sell programs, services, or products to communities of color.

Insights from a marketing professional of color

ON INSPIRING LEADERS WHO WALK THE TALK: I'm an African American woman marketing leader who was born and raised in the Twin Cities, the daughter of Nigerian immigrants to the United States. I have experienced the good, the bad, and the ugly of diversity in corporate culture throughout my career. I have experienced leaders who have participated in DEI initiatives to check a box; leaders who have been champions in the background, but were not bold enough to lead from the front; and leaders who have partnered with other CEOs to bring diversity and inclusion to the forefront of how they conduct their business and build their culture.

I have had the privilege of working closely with the CEOs at two wonderful Fortune 500 companies, and both have publicly championed diversity, equity, and inclusion. My biggest lesson in the importance of leadership support of DEI efforts came when I accepted my current position at a global retail company. **Our then-CEO spoke at the Twin Cities Black Affinity Network Development Day, which is an event hosted by five of the largest corporations in the Upper Midwest and offers programming for African Americans at all levels to participate in professional development targeted to them. His presence was important, and it was genuine.** He stayed the whole day, spoke with the participants and speakers, and from there, took a stand to really hold his executive team accountable for how DEI shows up, starting at the top.

ADVICE FOR CORPORATE LEADERS: If I were to speak to any CEO or group of CEOs, the advice I would give to them would be this: if you, as a leader, are serious about making DEI a priority, top-down accountability is the only way to make these values a part of your organization's culture. What does accountability mean?

- Have the tough conversations; enable leaders to learn so they can become teachers to their teams; empower them to Lead Out Loud with purpose to enrich their organization's culture.
- Encourage CEOs to ensure DEI is not just an initiative to build inclusiveness within your organization, but is also a part of your organization's culture, values, and business.
- Hold leaders accountable for the inclusion of DEI in all aspects of business and culture, just as they are held accountable to reach business or financial goals. When business goals are not met, there are consequences; the same standard should be held for DEI.
- Hire leaders that are passionate, bold, and serious about this work. Doing so will increase the retention of diverse employees and evolve the culture of your organization.

While scrolling through articles on LinkedIn, I came across a quote from Pat Wadors, Chief Talent Officer at ServiceNow. She said, "When we listen and celebrate what is both common and different, we become wiser, more inclusive, and better as an organization." I completely agree.

DEI is no longer optional for corporations. It is mandatory to ensure that employees feel welcome, know that they're part of your story, and see that they're participants in your organization's legacy.

Insights from an international business professional of color

ON DISTRIBUTION OF TALENT OF COLOR: I've noticed a lot of talk and not necessarily a lot of *walk* among the organizations where I've worked. And in the end, I've been able to use that knowledge to make some bold asks. If I'm throwing my name in for a new project or position, I can say, "Hey, if one of your goals in this work is to focus on diversity and inclusion, I can provide value in that area. I can contribute to that."

I would like to see more companies recognize that people of color belong everywhere within company org charts. I want them to see that not only are people of color as insanely talented as others within an organization, but also that **people of color need to be placed throughout all levels of an organization in order to achieve any DEI goals.** And, anyone moved into a leadership position will need consistent support. Those goals cannot be achieved by hiring a bunch of people of color from the lower ranks of the company, and then thrusting them into leadership without training or help. Prioritizing DEI means advancing them and supporting them all the way throughout their careers, and all the way throughout their journey at your company.

And, of course we need to get away from what feels like tokenism in DEI tactics. When you see only one or two people of color in a department or division, it feels obvious that they're there to fill a quota. Hard numerical diversity inclusion goals are important. But beyond being representative of the population, leaders need to look deeper into where talent of color is congregating, and where they're comfortable. They need to investigate if groups of professionals of color are concentrated in certain departments, and if that is what they want throughout their companies.

ADVICE FOR CORPORATE LEADERS: Leaders need to engage in more community outreach and invest in the betterment of the communities around them. Doing this can help create more opportunities for people of color through educational programs and trainings, setting them up so they can be qualified for those high, prominent positions. Community outreach, education, and empowerment efforts also remove the excuses, things like, "People of color aren't applying," or "Our recruitment efforts aren't working." **Instead of focusing solely on recruitment, focus on helping promising talent of color early on.** Fund school outreach programs, provide business training, offer professional development opportunities for talented young people of color.

Forget the rubrics, embrace the relationships

I love the honest stories and direct advice these professionals have shared. Every individual will have different experiences, of course, but I'm sure you saw themes emerging. So many of these talented people said they value honesty, follow-through, and accountability in their employers. They also said they want to see more leaders setting concrete DEI goals, creating failsafe plans to eradicate bias, and moving people of color into leadership roles. They all come from different backgrounds and offer different perspectives, but they're also united in their desire to help organizations be more effective in their efforts to include and empower professionals of color.

Another common thread among this feedback is the importance of relationships, and I agree wholeheartedly. I've always said it is crucial for business leaders to build strong, intentional, meaningful relationships with people who don't look like us, with people who don't make as much money as we do, and with people whom we normally wouldn't interact with. Being deliberate about our relationships doesn't just mean rubbing elbows with other execs; it means having a cup of coffee with a person who just spent fifteen years in prison. It means learning about other religions and belief systems. It means having conversations and asking questions and cultivating curiosity, so we are in a constant state of learning about other people. All of this makes a huge difference in how we run our organizations.

Many of my friends are White and we often throw small gatherings together, and even co-host annual holiday events. Our goal is to make sure that we're bringing people together who wouldn't normally meet each other. The truth is that most White people in my circle can live their entire lives without having a true, close friend of color, and I think that's downright tragic. So, we throw these events to bring people together because we believe that if people are connecting over meals and cocktails, they can get to know each other, have access to each other's networks, get comfortable seeing each other as friends and peers.

By creating these social opportunities, we can begin to change this narrative around networks and connections. Since leaders tend to hire based on personal referrals, and since personal networks tend to be homogeneous, there's a vicious cycle. We're trying to change that. When White leaders befriend leaders of color, when networks become more organically heterogeneous, it becomes easier to diversify leadership across industries. That's right, we throw events with not-so-hidden DEI agendas! And let me tell you, it WORKS.

My friends and I practice subtle bias-busting in other ways, too. Our parties often include people who have been incarcerated, women and men who experience a *much* harder time than most securing employment. These guests will mingle and have cocktails with executives and CEOs, including corporate leaders who generally refuse to hire people with criminal backgrounds, and when they get the full story it forces them to change the narrative. Having a conversation with a convicted felon who has been released, who's paid his debt to society and doesn't look like or act like or sound like all the stereotypes is eye-opening. We facilitate those connections because we want to change the tape that people play in their heads. We all have inherent prejudices, inherent biases, and sometimes we need to meet someone who reflects our biases back at us before we're ready to admit those preconceived thoughts are useless and outdated.

Throughout this book I have told you that DEI work is all about relationships. To create a culture of inclusivity, you need to get to know the diverse people in your sphere. Make friends with people who don't look like you. Learn their stories. Invite new people into your home. Share experiences together. Forge relationships with other leaders, but also with direct reports. Listen, learn, and connect.

For your next assignment, I want to encourage you to have a cup of coffee each week with a staff member or employee or fellow leader. Someone that you've met but don't really know yet, and someone who is very, very different from you. Be intentional about getting to know your team members, connecting with your middle managers, and showing up in your corporate community.

And once you've committed to a regular practice of one-on-one relationship-building within your company, consider your other activities as a leader. Where are you going for your speaking engagements? What media appearances are you making? Which charitable events are you attending? Who is in your friend circle? Who are you inviting to lunch? Who are you inviting to your home, and who are you inviting to your cabin? Who are you inviting to your birthday celebration, and who are you inviting to your holiday celebration? What does your golfing buddy list look like?

These relationship-building practices will enrich your life, I promise. You'll learn things and gain new perspectives. You'll be better equipped to view tough situations with compassion, and to ask those tough but thought-provoking questions of your new friends, questions that might have intimidated you to ask before. And, of course, your new friends can ask questions of you.

When you model diverse friendships as a leader, you give people permission to have open and candid conversations about what's going on with them, what's happening in their work lives. You can further facilitate those open conversations by hosting roundtables or town halls inside of your organization, where you attend as CEO specifically to listen and learn. Build spaces where you get close to the people you are trying to serve and help.

Bryan Stevenson, author of *Just Mercy*, says, "You can't understand most of the important things from a distance. You have to get close." I believe that. Proximity is crucial. When we get closer to people that we're not used to being close to—touching them, talking to them, having coffee with them—things change. Magic happens. We find clarity, and we change the world together.

Anyone who offers you a DEI checklist isn't just lying to you about how this work works; they're cheating you out of the very best part. Getting to know the diverse people within your company, understanding their lives and histories, is the single most rewarding thing an inclusion-minded leader can do. Forget about building some cut-and-dried, benchmark-driven, five-year plan to make your company a regional DEI superstar. Start by diversifying your own network. Start by having conversations with people who look nothing like you. Start with a cup of coffee.

At the beginning, that's really all it takes.

BUILDING RELATIONSHIPS

Richard Davis

Reba Dominski

James Burroughs II

Jay Lund

Greg Cunningham

Dr. Reatha Clark King

Pat McAdaragh

Ann McGlennen

Hubert Joly

Jennie Carlson

Karen Richard

AFTERWORD

For years, Andersen Corporation was *that* company. A company with good intentions. A company with a long history of striving to do the right thing. A company focused on building a high-performing team yet missing the mark when it came to attracting and retaining diverse talent.

Let me tell you, it's not because we didn't try. We did try. And, over the years, we became frustrated because we were so committed yet we struggled to make meaningful progress. Why were we having trouble hiring more talent of color and adding more diversity to our corporate leadership? **Our goals were straightforward and logical, but achieving them often felt challenging and overwhelming.**

When I began working with Sharon Smith-Akinsanya, many of our conversations centered around that fact that despite being fundamentally simple, DEI initiatives are incredibly complex. This complexity arises because we live in a global society that's moving through a massive cultural transition: becoming more divisive rather than inclusive.

As the leader of a fast-growing company navigating these complexities, I knew it was crucial for me to reaffirm Andersen's values, beliefs and direction as a company. My voice needs to be heard and my actions must make it crystal clear that Andersen is fully committed to a cultural shift that truly supports and encourages inclusivity. It's my job to be a thought-leader on DEI within the company.

Sharon calls this "Leading Out Loud." And we, as leaders, must be heard. Our messages must resonate throughout our organizations loud and clear—especially on difficult topics like race and equity. Because silence creates a void, and voids get filled with guesses, assumptions and misinformation about what's important to an organization.

Our company's views on diversity, equity and inclusion start with me, but they also must be upheld by every member of our executive committee, senior leadership team and board of directors. To create authentic cultural transformation from the inside out, these leaders must remain open to new ideas and be ready to challenge the status quo. I am proud to say that Andersen's leaders are all in.

Karen Richard, our chief human resources officer, and I have partnered to make some real changes, and while we still have a long way to go, in just one year we made some amazing progress. We also expanded our leadership team to help us move faster. We created a new Director of Diversity, Equity and Inclusion role, which we filled by promoting a diverse leader, and we brought in a diverse executive who had in-depth leadership experience in both talent acquisition and DEI.

Today, I am happy to report we are no longer *that* company. Yes, we still have a long way to go, but we are on a journey toward becoming a more diverse, equitable, and inclusive company. Fortunately, our journey is now moving at an accelerated pace.

Karen and I both agree that Sharon's guidance, coaching and connections exponentially expedited our ability to fill our talent pipeline with the right candidates. Sharon is a proponent of showing up everywhere we can in an authentic way to ensure we are meeting and building meaningful relationships with Andersen's "future leaders." We are following her advice and couldn't be more pleased with the results. And, this is just the beginning.

While many of the changes we have undertaken have involved modeling values and creating new roles, we also had to change *how we thought about DEI*. Like many companies, when Andersen first started talking about diversity, we saw it as a problem to solve. Now, we realize this was the wrong mindset.

Diversity, equity, and inclusion are not problems to solve, but opportunities to seize. Harnessing the full potential of a diverse workforce by listening to different points of view, benefiting from different experiences, and getting people to be more open-minded will advance the entire company. In fact, it will bring us all to a better place than we could ever reach with a homogeneous culture.

Here again, this relatively simple and straightforward mindset shift is one that takes time and effort to implement. But that's okay, because my leadership team and I also know that DEI work isn't a project—it's a journey. And small changes in our approach can unlock the simplicity within all that complexity to have the biggest impact. For example, we had been focusing on attracting diverse talent, but that wasn't enough. It was equally important to build a culture that was welcoming and inclusive, and then to share our story.

In hindsight, we know that fear was also standing in our way of making real progress. We were afraid to say the wrong thing, do the wrong thing, or ask the wrong questions. **We were eager to talk about change and make bold proclamations, but we were too cautious in taking bold action.** We had the best intentions but weren't leveraging them in the right ways.

I'd like to share a story that illustrates one way we have applied what we have learned. Sharon encourages CEOs to diversify their friend groups—to think about who they call to celebrate their wins, who they invite to social networking events, and with whom they share their knowledge, time and connections. One way to facilitate this is for CEOs to host leadership dinners at their homes. I thought this sounded intriguing, so I decided to give it a try, inviting everyone from some of Andersen's emerging leaders of color to the Mayor of St. Paul, Minnesota, to gather at my home.

These dinners have given me a chance to talk with my own employees on a deeper, more personal level, in an informal environment. They also provide Andersen's leaders with a new opportunity to meet promising employees they may not otherwise have had the chance to hear from, listening to their ideas and experiences, and building goodwill that extends far beyond the dinners. Through the dinners, I've also been able to connect with leaders of color in my community, and to build personal relationships that could lead to improved collaboration on innovative and life-changing initiatives.

Interestingly, it was more than just bringing people together for a dinner that made this program a success. Sharon has helped us see that there are very specific steps to take to curate experiences that are effective, meaningful and positive for all attendees (including myself!). For this program, opening my home to a wider, more diverse group of people was vitally important to the overall impact. **As leaders, we should be facilitating ways for people who don't look like each other, who are from a variety of socioeconomic backgrounds, to come together more often.**

This example is just one of dozens of stories and experiences I could share about the progress we are making at Andersen. Our journey is a powerful illustration of the principles outlined in this book being put into action. And, as a leader, action is your challenge.

Once you have made a commitment to diversity, equity and inclusion—to transformation, opening minds, and getting the work done—the next step is action. **What can you do to spark meaningful change within your company in the coming quarter, or year, or decade?** Can you commit to ensuring a higher percentage of new hires are diverse? Can you set goals to diversify your C-suite? Can you get a Diversity and Inclusion Council up and running? Now is the time to set DEI stretch-goals for yourself and your leadership team.

Why? Because failing to do so will leave your company behind. Remaining homogenous will ultimately cause you to lose your competitive edge and negatively impact your bottom line. You'll be missing out on transformative ideas on the leadership side, innovative thinking on the employee side, and valuable consumer interest on the buyer side. Without DEI at its heart, your organization is in danger of being outpaced and outperformed by more forward-thinking competitors.

Not only that, but **cultivating a company that is diverse, equitable, and inclusive is simply the right thing to do.** When we, as individuals, leaders, companies, and as a society, commit to advancing diversity, equity and inclusion, we begin the process of building a better future together. Yes, there will be plenty of complexities along the way, but the goal is fundamentally simple at its core. All we need is a willingness to do what's right.

Thank you for taking the time to read this book, for considering your important role in this cultural transformation, and for committing to meaningful change. I hope that you will take every single lesson in this book to heart, kick-start changes in your own company, and join me in building that better future. Starting today.

—**Jay Lund**, Chairman and CEO,
Andersen Corporation

GET THE HELP YOU NEED

We've come to the end . . . but it's actually just the beginning.

Which may sound disheartening because—if you've taken the time to read this whole book—you're not exactly a rookie. You've likely done a ton of research and reading, had some challenging discussions around diversity and race, and maybe even worked your butt off to spark change within your own organization. But you picked up this book because something still hasn't clicked within your company. Perhaps you're frustrated because you can't quite get people on board or find ways to shift internal viewpoints. There's a missing puzzle piece and you've been searching for it everywhere.

Every company is different, of course, but in my experience working with Fortune 500 companies and coaching their leaders, that missing piece is often ACTION. It can be uncomfortable and awkward to shift from talking about DEI to putting that talk into practice, but that's often the crucial next step. This includes taking responsibility, never passing the buck, and never again saying, "Oh, just let HR figure it out." It also includes making sure the board, the entire C-level, and all your direct reports have bought in. All the while, you need to be vocal, visible, and enthusiastic, so the whole company knows where you stand on DEI and social change.

It's a lot, I know. And if you're not sure how to do it, that's perfectly okay. Just *ask for help.*

There are experts and consultants and coaches out there just waiting for your call. They want to help you create strategies and build custom programs that will transform the ways your organization views talent of color and approaches issues of diversity. Heck, my own company, Rae Mackenzie Group, exists to help corporations build stronger and more authentic relationships to attract, recruit, and retain professionals of color. I've dedicated my entire career to supporting leaders just like you. And *even I* had to ask for help at one point.

Years ago, I sat down with Pat McAdaragh, President and CEO of Midco, and told him about my dream. I said that companies all over the country were grappling with issues of bias, failing to hire qualified professionals of color, and excluding people who should be included. I told him I wanted to change this. All of it. I wanted to find ways to help organizations do better, hire differently, prioritize DEI in meaningful ways. I wasn't sure how, but I knew I could do it . . . if I could just find someone to back me up.

As it turned out, Pat had hit a wall with his own diversity efforts at Midco. He wasn't finding the diverse pool of candidates he wanted, he wasn't sure how to change that, and he was ready to get creative. As we sat there talking during our lunch, he told me our meeting had to be some sort of a sign. Pat had known me for a grand total of 90 minutes, and he said, "You know what? I believe in you, and I'd like to take this DEI journey with you."

He told me that Midco was all in, that he'd partner with me by giving his advice, as well as his financial sponsorship. He said he had faith that changing the way corporations viewed DEI was a business imperative, and that he was thrilled to have found an expert in me.

It's a good thing you're reading this story, because if I had to tell it to you in person? I guarantee I'd be ugly crying by now. I am still so moved to know that Pat was willing to believe in me, to invest in me, to support me wholeheartedly after just one conversation. It felt scary and vulnerable to ask for his help, but he rewarded my gamble by giving me more encouragement than I imagined possible. And he's been a trusted partner ever since.

Diversity work is nuanced and difficult. Anything that involves racial inequity is overwhelming and emotional. *But it must get done.* And you, as a corporate leader, must take responsibility for getting it done. But you don't need to do that alone! Connect with local experts, call in your allies, tap talented DEI leaders and facilitators to help you make a plan and dive into action! Find the support and expertise you need to transform YOUR company! While it's true that CEOs and board members need to lead by example, they don't need to lead in isolation.

Hard work is made easier when we do it together. I know that from personal experience. **If you've found this book helpful but want some custom support in your company's DEI journey, I'd love to work with you.**

Thank you for taking the time to read these pages, and I sincerely hope what you've read has given you the tools, the guidance, and the momentum you need to start transforming your company into one that attracts and retains top talent of color. Thank you for having the bravery and foresight to push beyond DEI conversations and into transformative action. Thank you for learning to Lead Out Loud, so that other leaders may follow in your trailblazing footsteps.

TAKE THE NEXT STEP

Congratulations! You've read every insight-packed page of COLORFULL! Leaders like you who are constantly evolving, expanding, and educating are the ones who drive meaningful change in our world.

It's clear that we share the same values . . . AND it looks like you need a source to attract, recruit, and retain talent of color to maintain your competitive edge. I'd love to be that source for you and your company! I can bring in the diverse points-of-view that your organization needs to remain competitive in the workplace. I can provide custom guidance to your entire leadership team.

Get the actionable advice you've been searching for by partnering with me and my team at the Rae Mackenzie Group. Not only will we help you connect with your ideal hires, we'll also prepare your organization to welcome and retain the talent you're seeking. There's nothing worse than finding the perfect person for the job only to lose them weeks or months later. We're here to make sure you keep your talented employees of color, saving you both time and money.

When we work together, you will discover how to become a magnet in the marketplace for professionals of color. You'll learn:

- The right places to connect with professionals of color.
- How to turn your weakness around finding diverse talent into a strength.
- Why professionals of color are leaving your workplace, costing you thousands, and how to fix it.
- How to take the yawn out of your company profile and attract top professionals of color.
- How you and other leaders in your company can make yourselves more attractive to professionals of color online.
- How to successfully build authentic relationships with people who don't look like you.
- How to become a People Of Color Careers™ Equity Hiring and Advancement Partner (EHAP).
- And so much more!

Ready to take action?

Visit raemackenziegroup.com and schedule your discovery session. Let's create lasting change *together*.

ABOUT THE AUTHOR

Sharon Smith-Akinsanya is a force of nature whose life's work is to foster connectivity between corporations and people of color by helping employers attract and retain professionals of color with genuine inclusivity and opportunity to thrive. Her proven successes are why companies refer to her as their "secret weapon."

Sharon is an equity mentor, a diversity guru, and an anti-bias whisperer. She has an innate ability to address difficult topics without blame or shame. Her authenticity drives powerful, meaningful conversations on diversity, equity, and inclusion that many leaders never thought possible. Always a compelling speaker and instructor, Sharon can convince the most intractable audience to be more open-minded, even in the face of their own discomfort.

From her early years as a media sales rep in markets that ignored Black consumers to creating media strategies for the legendary musician Prince, Sharon's vast expertise includes decades of honing strategy, attaining high-level results, and producing events with flawless execution.

Today, Sharon is the founder of the People Of Color Careers™ social hiring network and the People Of Color Career Fair™, and CEO of Rae Mackenzie Group, Inc., Minnesota's top diversity, equity, and inclusion marketing firm. Her work with Fortune 500 companies, non-profits, and top employers like U.S. Bank, Best Buy, Midco, Andersen Windows & Doors, Thrivent, Make-A-Wish® America, and more centers on providing corporations with insight on how to prioritize cultural connectivity as part of their retention strategy. By doing so, not only do companies strengthen relationships with current employees, but they also open opportunities to talent of color.

Sharon believes in sparking big change from the inside out—and getting big results. Her innovative ideas create impactful opportunities for all involved. Through People Of Color Career Fair™ and PeopleOfColorCareers.com, Sharon turned her desire to connect professionals of color with life-changing careers into a wildly successful in-person and year-round digital hiring event supported by top political and business leaders in the region.

Although Sharon's firm focuses on initiatives in the Minneapolis-St. Paul Region, she firmly believes that by solving problems in her own backyard, she and her clients can lead by example. She wants the companies she supports to become DEI rock stars, showing other top corporations how to take the journey.